T0266734

QUANTUM
MEMORY
POWER

QUANTUM MEMORY POWER

LEARN TO IMPROVE YOUR MEMORY
WITH THE WORLD MEMORY CHAMPION!

DOMINIC O'BRIEN

MEDIA

Published 2020 by Gildan Media LLC
aka G&D Media
www.GandDmedia.com

Copyright © 2020 by Dominic O'Brien

No part of this book may be used, reproduced or transmitted in any manner whatsoever, by any means (electronic, photocopying, recording, or otherwise), without the prior written permission of the author, except in the case of brief quotations embodied in critical articles and reviews. No liability is assumed with respect to the use of the information contained within. Although every precaution has been taken, the author and publisher assume no liability for errors or omissions. Neither is any liability assumed for damages resulting from the use of the information contained herein.

First Edition: 2020

Front cover design by David Rheinhardt of Pyrographx

Interior design by Meghan Day Healey of Story Horse, LLC.

Library of Congress Cataloging-in-Publication Data is available upon request

ISBN: 978-1-7225-0324-6

10   9   8   7   6   5   4   3   2   1

Contents

. . . .

Foreword

Dominic O'Brien was not born with a special gift for memorizing vast amounts of information. Yes, he has won the World Memory Championships a record 8 times and is the current Senior World Champion as well as being in the record books for memorizing 54 decks of playing cards after a single sighting of each card. He can memorize a random sequence of 2,000 numbers in less than an hour and appears regularly on television, memorizing anything from shopping lists to the names and faces of an entire audience.

Yet Dominic is only able to accomplish these feats because he has trained his brain to do them. What he can do, you can do too. The techniques, systems, and strategies in *Quantum Memory Power* are unrivaled. They are the most powerful in the world, and the reason is simple: Dominic has devised each and every method from his own trials and errors. The systems that worked, he kept and refined. Those that were unproductive, he discarded. The result is a powerful system, the Dominic System, that will unleash quantum memory powers you never knew you had.

You'll learn to remember names, faces, numbers, birthdays, dates, appointments, speeches, or any sequence of numbers you want. Once you have unleashed your memory power, there will be no limits to the type or quantity of information you will be able to store. With each powerful technique in *Quantum Memory Power*, you'll be given practical applications and exercises to test and strengthen your abilities in each area.

You'll be using your imagination and creative abilities in ways you never imagined to gain speed, accuracy, and poise in the development of your own special quantum memory powers. Not only will you learn how to develop a powerful memory, but you'll gain competence and self-esteem.

You'll learn how your brain operates, how to improve your decision making powers, how to remember directions, how to develop laser-sharp concentration, and everything from acing a tough job interview to developing a mental fact file.

You're about to take the journey of a lifetime. You never realized that learning could be such fun. Who knows? You could end up challenging Dominic at the next World Memory Championship.

1

It's Time for Mental Fitness

· ·

ogether we're going to take a quantum leap in unleashing the true potential of your memory. We're going to unlock a wealth of memory power that you probably didn't even know that you had.

How would you like to remember the names and faces of everybody you meet and store that information in your memory, not just for days and weeks, but for months and years ahead?

I'm going to take you on a journey through the world of mnemonics, and I'm going to teach you a new language—the language of numbers—so that you'll be able to remember any number—dates, birthdays, appointments, telephone numbers. Now I'm talking big numbers here: 50 digits, 100, maybe even 1,000 or more.

How would you like to be able to deliver a lengthy speech entirely from memory, with no notes at all? I'm going to teach you how to do that. I'll also teach you how to remember quotes, anecdotes, jokes, and material that will impress even the coldest of audiences.

Imagine reading through a newspaper or magazine and being able to remember every single detail in it. You'll even be able to pinpoint the exact detail on any page. That'll impress your family and friends.

How would you like to pinpoint the day of the week for any date in the last century? Not just the last century, but any date in the future or in the past. You'll be able to do that in seconds.

I'm going to teach you the secrets of accelerated learning. Maybe you're a student, or perhaps you have children studying at school. I'm going to teach you how to learn so that you can absorb knowledge the lazy man's way. You're going to learn new words. You won't make spelling mistakes anymore. I'll even teach you how to learn a vocabulary in a foreign language. That's just the beginning.

In the advanced section of this book, I'm going to teach you how to master your own brain waves. I'm going to teach you how to control both sides of your brain. You could be a walking Einstein without evening know it. I'm even going to teach you how to memorize, not one deck of cards, but several. In short, I'm going to groom you to become a memory champion in your own right.

At the moment, you're probably thinking, "Maybe this guy can teach me a thing or two, but I bet he was born with a very special brain. Maybe he has a photographic memory."

You'd be absolutely wrong. In fact at school I was described as dyslexic. I left school when I was 16. Here are some actual reports from when I was a child. Age 9½: "Calculation terribly slow, must concentrate, often cannot repeat the question." I was 19th out of a class of 22.

Here's another. Age 10¼: "He tends to dream in the middle of a calculation, which leads him to lose track of the thought." I was 17th out of a class of 23.

This is my favorite one. "Geography: has not paid much attention. Appears to know more of the universe than the earth."

From those school reports, you wouldn't think there was a future memory champion in the making, would you? It was only in 1987, when I saw a guy on television memorize a deck of cards, that the way I thought about my own memory was transformed.

In the World Memory Championships, you have to listen to a 200-digit number spoken at the rate of 1-digit per second. The person that can memorize the most digits before making a mistake is the winner. In other words, it's sudden death. I was able to memorize the first 128 digits. You can do this too.

THE WORLD MEMORY CHAMPIONSHIPS

Let me give you a little bit of the background of the World Memory Championships. They started in 1991, and ever since then their numbers have grown. We have national champions: a United States champion, a German, Malaysian, English, Irish, Turkish champion, and so on. The best of each country all gather each year in London for the world championship.

This is the very first examination; it's 1 of 10 events on a Thursday morning. We all sit down, all 400 of us, and we're confronted with a number. We have 1 hour to memorize just 1 number. Not too difficult, you might think, but this particular number is 3,000 digits long, and it's randomly generated. You have to read through the number like a book and memorize as many of the digits as possible.

There are penalties. On the first page, you have 25 rows of 40 digits. If you make a mistake on the first line, then you lose 20 digits. If you make 2 or more mistakes, then you lose the whole line. Last year I tried to memorize 1,820. My best, after penalties, is 1,780 digits.

In the next test, you're given 100 names and faces that you've never seen before, and you have 15 minutes to memorize them. You get a 500-word poem to memorize. You have an hour to memorize as many decks of cards as you can. I usually attempt over twenty decks. Last year, I did 18½ decks. Here's one of the more quirky ones: you get half an hour to memorize 3,000 binary digits. The person who can memorize the most information altogether wins the championships.

At this point you're probably thinking, "What a sad man. This guy should get out more often." You probably think that all I do all day long is just sit and stare at loads of numbers and playing cards. Well, I don't, unless I'm in training a couple of months before the championships.

People often ask me, "What is the point in trying to memorize a 2,385-digit binary number? It doesn't get you anywhere, does it?"

Here's the answer I normally give: why would 22 fully grown men want to kick a ball from one end of a field to get it into a net at the other? Why should a fully grown man or woman want to hit a little white ball from the top of a hill to get it into a little tin cup 300 yards down the other end of the field? There's no point, is there? It's hardly crucial to survival. When you go to bed, you don't tell your wife, "OK, dear. Make sure that the cat's out, the fire alarm is on, and the ball is at the back of the net."

We don't need to survive that way. The point is not the ball being in the back of the net, but how it gets there. That's the fascination, the skill, the artistry, and there's a whole industry behind it.

The order of a deck of cards in my head is not the point, but rather how it gets there. Not only is it fascinating, it's an extremely beneficial skill. Just think what you could do with that skill if you had it, and I'm going to teach you.

There are some side effects, but they're all positive. You'll begin to develop a laser-sharp concentration. You'll find that as your memory develops, your confidence increases. Stress levels will come down. You'll get a wider range of observation. You'll become more creative and more imaginative. It only takes a few minutes of practice each day, and you don't have to be a nuclear scientist to be able to do this stuff.

A few years ago, when I was writing my first book on memory, I wanted to put a patent out on the techniques and systems that I developed, because I believe they're the most powerful that you can use to develop your memory. It came as a shock to find that someone had gotten there before I did. In fact, I was 2,000 years out. I discovered that the Greeks had already developed very similar techniques, because they were living in an oral culture. They didn't have any paper, although they had papyrus and parchment: crude forms of paper. If their culture was to survive, it had to be passed on by word of mouth. This required people of the day to have very good memories. If they didn't have these naturally, they had to use artificial devices so they would be able to record stories of battles and the details of politics. They would be able to talk for hours and hours on end. They used a technique called *mnemonics*.

At that time, the Greeks had some of the greatest minds the world has ever seen. Since then, we've had the development of paper. We have the printing press. We now have the world's biggest library, the Internet, so there's a lot of knowledge that we don't need to store in our heads.

I don't want to go back to Greek times. I'm very happy with the amount of knowledge that we have in computers, the Internet, and everything else, but maybe what we've gained in efficiency has come at the expense of mental agility. We don't have to work our brains quite so hard.

Have you noticed that over the past two or three decades there's been a surge of body fitness videos? Actors and athletes keep bringing them out. We've learned that to stay young, healthy, and happy, it's a good idea to look after our bodies. Great advice—I could do with losing a couple of pounds myself. We don't necessarily heed that advice, but at least we know about it. We have government promotions that say, "Why don't you take half an hour of physical exercise every day, whether it's walking the dog or cycling to work instead of driving—something that leaves you a little out of breath?"

I think there should be a government health campaign encouraging us to take half an hour or even 10 minutes of mental exercise every day—something that leaves our brains slightly out of breath.

I'm going to be giving you plenty of these exercises in this book. You can regard it as a training manual for the brain. I want you to regard me as your personal memory fitness trainer.

2

Three Keys to Quantum Memory Power

The techniques, systems, and strategies that I'm going to reveal to you are, in my opinion, unrivaled. After all, I needed something that was going to make me win the World Memory Championships.

I devised each and every method from my own trials and errors. I kept and refined the systems that worked and threw out those that didn't, so a kind of natural selection took place. I'm only reluctant to reveal these techniques because you might be the one person that uses them to beat me at the World Memory Championships. If you do, I hope that you'll at least acknowledge it at the awards ceremony.

I want to know exactly what your memory span is at the moment, so that we can compare it with

results later on. I'm going to give you a couple of
very simple tests.

I'm going to give you a series of 10 words. The
idea is to remember as many words as you can in
order before you make a mistake. Maybe you won't
make a mistake.

Get a pencil and paper. First, read this list carefully:

Sand	Rope
Flashlight	Card
Bathtub	Lion
Football	River
Gnome	Target

Now close the book and write down as many as
you can. Once you're finished, open the book up
again, read the list, and see how many you have
right.

How did you do? Just make a note. It doesn't
matter if you made mistakes. Maybe you only got
one right, but by the end of this course, I'm willing
to bet you'll get all 10 in order, backwards or forwards.

We have one more test, a number test. Here are
14 digits: 6, 8, 0, 2, 8, 6, 0, 8, 9, 1, 7, 4, 3, 5

Again, take a pencil and paper. Read this list
of numbers carefully and remember as many as you

can. Then close the book and write down the numbers you remember, in the correct sequence.

How many numbers did you remember? How many did you get right? Maybe you made a mistake on the second digit, in which case, your score is 1 (because you only got 1 right in order).

We're not looking for perfection here. I don't expect you to memorize all 10 objects. This is the first exercise you've done, so like any underused muscle, your brain is bound to feel a bit stiff to begin with, but I'm giving you this to ease you into the course.

About a quarter of the way through, you'll find that all these exercises will come as second nature to you, so don't be disappointed if you've made a mess of it right now.

ALI

I'm going to give you three key ingredients for developing awesome powers of memory. You're going to be using these right throughout the course. They are *association*, *location*, and *imagination*.

Here's your first memory test. How are you going to memorize these three principles? If you take the first letter of each word, you come up with ALI. Think of Muhammad Ali, who said, "I am the greatest," because these are the greatest techniques.

Let's start off with *association*, which is the first golden key of memory. If I say *key*, you think of *door*. If I say *skiing*, you think of *snowman*. If I say *snowman*, you think of *Christmas*, and so on. What if I say *Tiger Woods*? You think of *golf*. *Monica Lewinsky*—OK, you get the picture.

Association works because in our minds, everything is connected to everything else. We identify something not by its dictionary definition, but by what we associate it with. If I say *bicycle*, you don't suddenly think, "Oh, yeah, that's a vehicle with two wheels, one directly in front of the other, driven by pedals." No, you think of 1,001 other things. You think about the first time you rode a bicycle, a birthday present, an accident. You think about the first time you tried to ride a bike yourself. I can remember being age 7 and getting a nice red bicycle for my birthday. It's everything but the dictionary definition.

Association is the mechanism, the cogs and wheels, the nuts and bolts by which memory works, and we're going to be using plenty of it.

Here's the first exercise. I'm going to give you 3 pairs of words or objects, and I want you to forge a link between each of them. There's not necessarily a ready-made link, so you're going to have to find one. For instance, if I say *kangaroo* and *masterpiece*, how are you going to connect those 2 words together? Think about it.

Introduce a bit of creativity. Maybe you were thinking of a masterpiece: a painting of a kangaroo. That's what most people would think, but I want you to get more creative. I want you to think outside the norm.

Let me give you 3 pairs of words now. See if you can make a connection on your own between them. Here we go. Here's the first pair: *bicycle, hamster.* The next pair: *balloon, submarine.* Finally: *palm tree, chocolate.*

If I asked you, what word is linked to *hamster?* you'd answer, *bicycle.* If I say *balloon,* what do you think of? Answer, *submarine.* If I say *chocolate,* what do you see? A *palm tree.*

It's simple, isn't it? Even though there wasn't a direct link between each word, it really wasn't that difficult to make an artificial connection between them.

From now on, I want you to get used to making associations. You should think of the first thing that comes into your head, because those things will end up being the most reliable.

I was doing a crossword this morning, and there was a clue for a five-letter and a four-letter word. It said, "Working hard, they're linked for some time." Immediately I thought of *link, chain,* and I came up with *chain gang.* So you may notice that if you start loosening the cogs of your memory and getting used to associations, it will help with things like crosswords.

The next golden key of memory is *location*. Location is like the map of memory. It's where you look in order to access all your stored memories. For instance, if I ask you to tell me everything you did yesterday in order, what will you start doing? What goes on in your head? You'll have to think of the places you were at. That's what keeps the order.

Let's make it more difficult. If I say to you, what happened at exactly this time last week? you really will have to start searching for the places you were at. We live in a 3D world. We can't dissociate our past from location.

Since I've been developing these techniques, I've been looking at other authors' work. They seem to miss out on this one thing—the use of location— but it's really in the true tradition of Greek method of memorization.

The third golden key of memory, which is probably the most important, is *imagination*. I call it the fuel of memory. We all possess imagination, although some people's are more wild than others'. If you believe you lack imagination, just think back to when you were a child playing imaginary games in the garden. Weren't you wonderfully creative with your mind?

You're going to need plenty of creative imagination in this course. Some people say that they're not imaginative and can't come up with ideas as fast as others. But it's not a case of learning creativity. It's not something that you can teach; it's more a case of encouraging its return.

I believe that we're all taught far too soon in our lives to grow up, to be sensible—"welcome to the real world"—and that can tend to stifle creativity. Fortunately, I refused to give up my creativity and imagination, which was probably the downfall of my academic success at school.

I've always possessed a vibrant imagination, but I never realized that it would be so instrumental in developing staggering powers of memory. You already have an extraordinary imagination: just think about the incredible dreams that you have in the night. From now on, you're going to use your imagination in ways that you never even imagined.

THE LINK METHOD

We're going to start with the first method for memorizing a list of objects in order. This is called the *link method*, or sometimes the *story method*.

We'll take the list that I gave you above, but this time, we're going to connect the words together using a story.

We're going to go through that list again:

Sand	Rope
Flashlight	Card
Bathtub	Lion
Football	River
Gnome	Target

To be able to remember that, we're going to connect the words together in a story. Just try to picture the scenes. Let them wash over you as I go through this little story, and put yourself in the scene as well.

Imagine walking along a sandy beach. *Sand* is the first word. Just feel the warm sand oozing between your toes. A little way ahead, there's a beam of light. Where is it coming from? It's coming from a *flashlight* stuck in the sand. You walk towards the flashlight, pick it up, and shine it. It shows a little white object in the distance. As you get further towards it, you see that that object is a *bathtub*, which is the next item on the list.

You walk up to the bathtub. Inside there's a big plastic *football*. You lift the football out, you kick it, and it lands on a little plastic *gnome* in the distance. Just make a note that the gnome has the number 5 on it, to remind you that it's the fifth item on the list.

You walk up to the gnome, and attached to it is a *rope*. Your curiosity gets the better of you, so you start pulling the rope. You start using it as a guide, and it leads you to a *card*, which is the seventh item on the list. To remember that, you notice that the card is a big card; it's about the size of you. It's the 7 of clubs.

Now this card turns into a *door*, and as you open the door, you see a *lion*. Maybe the lion is playing a card game. Because the lion is so startled at your arrival, it jumps out and lands in a *river*. Now picture the river going to a point in the distance, and that point in the distance is a *target*.

Now, using that powerful, abundant supply of imagination, go through that story again, and let's see if you can pick out the objects. Let me ask you a question to begin with; what was the seventh object on the list? It should be a card, shouldn't it? The 7 of clubs. If I ask, what was the fifth? you'll know it's the gnome. Now let's go through the whole list.

What was the first thing that happened? You're on a beach, so something is between your toes. It has to be *sand*. Then you noticed what? A beam of light. It has to be the *flashlight*. You picked up the flashlight, and you shone it on a white object in the distance. Got it? It's a *bathtub*. What was inside the bathtub? A big plastic *football*, which you took out and kicked, and which landed on a *gnome*. What was attached to the gnome? A *rope*.

Now you pulled on the rope, and it led you towards what? The *card*, the 7 of clubs which turned into a door, which you opened, and there was a *lion*. The lion was started and jumped where? Into the *river*, and the river went off to a point in the distance, which was a *target*.

All of a sudden, because you've used imagination and association, you've linked those words together in a story, and you can even go backwards. All you have to do is just reverse the story. So what do we have? Target, river, lion, card, and so on.

If you've never bought a book on memory training before, you might be thinking, "Hmm, that's a pretty neat way of memorizing a list." But if you have read a book on memory, the chances are that you're probably thinking, "I already know that method. I was looking for something different."

This method is used by trainers, presenters, magicians, and memory men and women. It does work, and I use it occasionally, but do you honestly think that I have time to devise a story when I try to memorize a deck of 52 playing cards in 30 seconds? Absolutely not. I just want to see and take a snapshot of each card as quickly as I can. I don't have time to make up connections like that.

I merely gave you that exercise as a warm-up to ease you into the next method, which is called the *journey method*, which you're going to get in chapter 3. Even so, maybe you memorized all 10 of those just using the story method. If so, it just shows you that once you start letting that imagination flow using association, your memory starts to work well for you. You're starting to develop quantum memory power.

3

The Journey Method

∙∙

n this chapter, I'm going to teach you a powerful method for learning a list of information. It could be anything from a shopping list to the elements of the periodic table.

First of all, I want you to go back to 1987, because that's when my life changed. Before then, if you'd have presented me with a 10-digit number, I probably would have gotten about 6 or 7 digits right. As for cards, I probably couldn't have memorized more than about 4 or 5 in sequence. So what happened in 1987 to change all that?

One day I was channel-surfing, and I saw an amazing man called Creighton Carvello, who was on a program called *Record Breakers*. He was attempting to memorize a deck of cards, which he did in just under 3 minutes.

Had I not seen that, I wouldn't have thought it was humanly possible, because the cards were dealt out one at a time, one on top of each other. I figured, "He's not actually photographically memorizing the cards; he must have a system for connecting one card to the next." But I really should have had more faith in his natural abilities.

So armed with a deck of cards, I went up to my room, and I decided to try it out for myself. I couldn't connect more than about 4 or 5 cards together. This got me thinking. I'd heard about making up a story, like the one I described in chapter 1, and using mnemonics, so I decided to give the cards a symbol, but first of all I thought, "I wonder if Creighton is using a trick here. Maybe he's using his body to store the information." Maybe he had a system by which, if the first card was the 2 of clubs, he would move his left foot to 2 o'clock. If the next card was the 3 of diamonds, he would move his right foot to 3 o'clock, so he'd gradually work his way up his body. Every time he dealt a card, one part of his body would have to move. The mind boggles, because 52 parts of his body would have to move in 52 separate ways.

So I threw that possibility out. Then I thought, "Perhaps there's some math here. Maybe he's using a calculation," but so far no one has come up with a method for that. I really should have focused more on human intuition, on memory power.

I'd recently been on a business trip to Khartoum, in the Sudan, and I'd been sitting around in a place called the Sudan Club, waiting for businessmen to come along (which they never did). In five weeks there, I got used to the layout of the Sudan Club. I knew exactly the layout of the restaurant, the swimming pool area, the squash court, and so on.

I thought that maybe if I turned each card into a person or an object, I could connect them by imagining them sitting around the swimming pool or in the restaurant. Then I thought, "Well, it's going to get a bit crowded, isn't it? If I have 52 objects, and 52 people are all mingling around in a big party, how am I going to get the sequence right?"

Then it suddenly hit me. Why didn't I just put them on a journey? Make up a journey of 52 stops or stages, right around the city of Khartoum, and then just walk through it and imagine seeing each card as a person or an object. This really was the eureka factor. This was my development of the journey method.

Here's what I want you to do. I don't want you to start thinking about memorizing anything. All I want you to do is form your own journey around your house. Start with the place where you wake up in the morning, your bedroom: that could be the first stage. Where do you go next? Maybe you go to the bathroom, so that would be the second stage; the spare room would be the third stage; the fourth stage, the staircase; and so on.

I don't know what your house is like, so you have to make up the journey yourself, but just count off 10 stages on your fingers.

If you really want to maximize the benefit of this, close your eyes and imagine the journey that way, because you avoid distractions. When I'm recording information or memorizing a spoken digit number, I always have my eyes closed. Try this with your eyes closed, because that will keep you from being distracted by the outside world. It helps you to focus on the information that you're receiving.

Imagine that you're floating through the house. Just get the feel of the house, as though you're there now, looking at all the familiar knickknacks. Gradually count off 10 stages on your fingers. If you run out of rooms, go into the yard. Maybe call the front gate one of the stages. If you run out of yard, go into the street or to the next-door neighbor's house. It doesn't really matter, but it is important that you keep an order through the journey. You wouldn't go from your bedroom to the garden shed to the upstairs bathroom (unless it was a Friday night and you had too much to drink).

When you have 10 stages, then we're ready to implement the journey method. It's most important that you lay down this order of stages. So prepare the journey, and the best way to do that is to put down this book now. When you have your stages ready, then open it up again.

If you have your 10 stages, then we're ready to lay down the information. I must say at the start that this is not a test of memory. This is going to be a demonstration of imagination, so don't consciously try to memorize anything at all. All I want you to do is just use your vibrant imagination, and just picture the images that come along.

Now when I say *imagination*, I don't simply mean forming images in your mind. I want you to use all the cortical skills that you have at your disposal. Use all your senses: sight, sound, smell, taste, and touch. Try to introduce movement; use exaggeration, humor, sex, anything you like so that your imagination can work.

Now move gradually from stage to stage, and I'm going to feed you some objects. Start at the beginning. You're in your bedroom. The first object I'm going to give you is a *wallet.*

Now use exaggeration. Give it position. What's it doing? Where is it? Perhaps it's a huge wallet, bulging with dollars, right at the end of your bed. Try to picture that. What's the wallet made of? Is it leather? Can you smell it? Use your senses.

Leave the wallet alone and move on to the second stage, wherever that might be. It could be your bathroom. The next object is a *snake*. Maybe you hate snakes, but it's a snake. Perhaps it's in the bath. What type of snake is it? Give it a color. Is it slimy? Just picture that. Use movement, exaggeration.

Now move on to the third stage of the journey, wherever you are now; it could be your spare room. The next object is a *screwdriver*. Use exaggeration. Make it outsized. Give it a position in the room. Use logic. Why is it there? Maybe you're doing some repairs in that particular room. What's the color of the screwdriver's handle? Maybe it's striped yellow and black.

Great. Leave the screwdriver. Move on to the next stage of the journey. This time the word is *peach*. Imagine a giant peach wherever you're standing now in your house. Pick it up. How heavy is it? Imagine tasting it. Maybe it has a little bit of fur on the side. Is it a fresh peach? Is it bruised, damaged? What does it taste of? Again, use all your senses.

Put the peach down, and move to the next stage. This time I want you to make a mental note that this is the fifth stage. The object is a *drum*. Obviously this time you're going to use sound. Imagine picking up a stick and banging the drum. How loud is it? Is it going to disturb the neighbors? Whereabouts is the drum in that particular room?

Again, use all your senses; sound and touch the drum, and remember that it's the fifth stage. You're halfway through the journey now.

Now move on to the next stage of the journey. The word here is *book*. Why would a book be in that particular place in your house? Maybe you're in the yard now. What sort of book is it? Is it a hardback? Is it softback? What color is it? What's the title?

Put the book down and move to the next stage. This time I want you to imagine a *piano*. Maybe you play the piano, or maybe there's a famous pianist playing it, maybe Liberace. What's he doing there? Use sound. What sort of music is he playing?

Move on to the next stage now. We're nearly at the end of the journey. This time I want you to imagine a *goat*. Just see it there. Walk up to it, touch it, feel it. Is it soft? Does it make a noise? Is it chewing? What color is it? What's it doing? Why should it be there? Use logic as well.

OK, leave the goat behind. This time, on the next stage of the journey, you see a *mirror*. What do you see in the mirror? Why is it there? Is it cracked? Do you make it crack?

Finally, at the very last stage of the journey, you see a *tank*. What is it? Is it an army tank or a water tank? I'll leave that up to you.

Great. As I said at the beginning, this is a demonstration of imagination. This is not a test of memory, but as I said, the three keys of memory are *imagination*, *association*, and *location*. I'm willing to bet if that you used all three, you should now be able to recall all 10 of those objects. (Don't worry if you can't to begin with. We'll ease you into this.)

Go back now to the first stage of your journey. Where were you? You were in the bedroom. There was something at the end of the bed. What was it? Maybe it's made of leather. That's right. It's the *wallet*, that thing oozing with dollars.

Then we went to the next stage. Maybe it's the bathroom. There was something in there. What was it? Something slimy. A *snake*. Great.

Next stage, wherever that is. What's in it? Maybe something having to do with repairs you were doing in the room. It's a *screwdriver*.

Move on to the next stage. Something that you tasted. A *peach*. Great.

Again, move on to the next stage. This has something to do with sound. Maybe you're worried about disturbing the neighbors. It's a big *drum*. What stage of the journey is it? Do you remember that I said to note that it's halfway through, so it's the fifth stage of the journey?

Move on. Wherever you are now, there was something that you were reading. It's a *book*.

Moving on. Who's there? Liberace. What's he doing there? Playing the *piano*.

Leave Liberace alone. Move on to the next stage, and you can see what? Clue: it's an animal. That's it. It's the *goat*.

We're nearly there. The next stage involves something to do with you, maybe a reflection. OK, that's the *mirror*.

Finally, the very last stage. What was it? Was it an army *tank* or a water tank?

How did you get on? Maybe you missed out on a few of the words, but don't worry if you did. All it means is that you didn't really make the images strong or stimulating enough. The answer is just to go back, review each scene, or reshoot it if you like. Don't blame the projectionist when the recording is faulty. Just go back and change a few of the images. Reshoot the scene.

Have you noticed that the journey beautifully preserves the order of the objects? So if I said to you, "What's the sixth object?" all you have to do is go back to the journey. You know where the fifth is, so you go one forward, and it's the book. We can do it the other way around. If I say to you, "Where on the list did the snake come?" you think back a minute. You had the wallet, and then you went to the bathroom, so it has to be the second on the list.

In fact, by using the journey, you could easily reverse the order of the items. Just reverse the journey. What was the last item? Think about it. Tank. Go back: mirror, goat, piano, book, and so on.

So all three aspects of memory are working beautifully together. *Imagination*—you're using plenty of that. You were *associating* the objects; you were thinking of them, exaggerating them, and putting them into *locations*, so all three qualities have worked together. That's why you can use them to great effect.

Obviously there are practical benefits to this process, but apart from anything else, it is a wonderful exercise for the whole of your brain. We'll be looking at brain function in later chapters.

I suggest you try an experiment: Write down a random list of 10 objects. You can get your family or friends to do this. Have them to call the objects out slowly, and see if you can memorize or just imagine each of them along a journey.

Of course, speed comes with practice, and after a while, you will be amazed at how easy this is to do. You won't be looking at 10 objects. You'll be wanting to do 20, 30, 50, maybe 100. These are all benefits of the journey method.

4

Revision and Review

. . . .

Y ou're already getting the hang of this. Your imagination is working well for you. You're successful in turning dull, unintelligible data into meaningful, colorful, memorable images, but now you're asking, "How long will this stuff stay in my head?"

Using imagery in this way is extremely powerful, but to consolidate a memory, to really set it in concrete for long-term storage, you must review those images. Revision and review are more or less the same thing.

Back in 1878, the German psychologist Hermann Ebbinghaus worked out that the best way to revise was to return to the information at least 5 times. Depending on the type of information, here is how I would split that revision time: Whatever you learn, review it immediately. That's the first review. Then look at it 24 hours later. Then, 1 week later; that's the third review. Then review it 1 month later, and then anywhere between 3 and 6 months later. If you can do the review in that sort of spread, then you'll pretty much have the information for life. That's the minimum. Obviously the more times you review the material, the better.

Another thing: take breaks. If the information is intense, try to take a short break every 20 minutes or so, but not for more than about 5 minutes. Do something completely different. Oddly enough, even though you're taking a rest, your brain is still starting to organize and process the information you've just been absorbing.

This phenomenon is called *reminiscence.* A memory steadily improves several minutes after we've learned something. The length varies depending on the type of information. To give you an example, your memory of a photograph is at its strongest about 1½ minutes after studying it. Memory of a manual skill, whether it's being taught how to hold a golf club or ride a bike, is usually better 10 minutes after practicing it.

Here's the point: if you distribute the learning periods over, say, 20 to 45 minutes, you will increase the number of reminiscence periods. In other words, you're going to learn more. Isn't that nice to know? If you keep taking breaks, you're going to learn more; even when you're making a cup of tea, you're still learning. I'll bet they never taught you that at school.

Experiment. Use all the devices available. Get your children onto this. Try it out with them. If you're a student, this technique could mean the difference between two grades—between success and failure. Furthermore, it doesn't take a genius to work out that if you double the rate at which you absorb knowledge, then you're going to halve your study time.

I mentioned earlier that the Greeks used this method to great effect. Later the Romans used it as well. Below is a passage from a text called *Ad Herennium* (To Herennius). It's from the first century BC. It's by an unknown author, who writes:

If we wish to remember much material, we must equip ourselves with a large number of places. It is essential that he places should form a series and must be remembered in their order so that we can start in any locus in the series, and move either backwards or forwards.

A locus is a place easily grasped by the memory, such as a house, an intercolumnar space, a corner, an arch, or the like. If we wish to remember, for instance, the genus of a horse, of a lion, of an eagle, we must place their images on definite loci.

I thought I had invented a completely unique method, but I suppose I have at least revived it for the 21st century.

5

Combining the Linking and Journey Methods

· ·

We're now going to take things one step further. How can you use the journey method to gain knowledge fast? I'm going to get you now to memorize a list of the 10 largest oceans and seas.

Pacific Ocean   South China Sea
Atlantic Ocean   Caribbean Sea
Indian Ocean   Mediterranean Sea
Arctic Ocean   Bering Sea
Arabian Sea   Bay of Bengal

If you cover this list, you'll find you've forgotten it, haven't you? Maybe you've remembered the first bit—the Pacific, Atlantic, Indian oceans—but to get them in order is pretty difficult.

Remember earlier that I said to find a connection between two words? Just think of an immediate association. That's what I want you to do. I want you to combine linking with the journey method.

When I say *Pacific*, what's the first thing that comes into your head? I think of a pack of cards: *Pacific, pack*. *Atlantic* makes me think of *atlas*. With *Indian*, I think of a Cherokee *Indian*. For *Arctic Ocean*, what do you think of? Maybe an *arc* or an *arch*.

We're going to memorize that list of oceans and seas. In order to do that, you have to have another journey of 10 stages. I don't want you to use the journey you've just formed around your house, because that method is so powerful that you still have those images in your head: the wallet, the snake, the screwdriver. This one has to be fresh. It could be a journey from your home to work, or it could be an old school trip that you used to take, or maybe a journey along a coastal resort.

Stop reading and work out another journey of 10 stages. Use a different place, maybe an old school trip or the layout of your office, or maybe a trip around the town center.

Once you have 10 stages of a very familiar journey, I'm going to try to ease those images into the background scenes.

Go to the first stage of your journey. The first body of water is the *Pacific Ocean*. The idea here is to associate *Pacific* with something. Earlier I suggested a *pack of cards*, so let's do that one together. Picture a pack of cards at that particular location. Maybe you're on a beach or at your old school. Wherever you are, picture a pack of cards. Remember to use all the cortical skills: your senses, movement, exaggeration, humor.

Leave the cards alone and go to the second stage. This time it's *Atlantic Ocean*. What do you connect with *Atlantic*? Why not try *atlas*? Try to picture a huge atlas. Again, use logic. Why would the atlas be there? Maybe someone's left it there, or they've dropped it, or maybe it's to help you find your way along the journey.

OK, leave the atlas alone. Go to the next stage: *Indian Ocean*. Imagine bumping into a Cherokee Indian. Use interaction here. What's the Cherokee doing there?

Move on. Next is *Arctic Ocean*. I would use an *arch*. Imagine walking through an archway. What's it made of? Plastic? Don't forget to use touch, taste, sight, smell, and sound. Imagine walking through the arch as you go to the next stage of your journey.

This time, *Arabian Sea*. Maybe the first thing that comes into your mind is an *Arabian* knight—a nice, colorful character. Picture that.

Now move on to the next stage: *South China Sea*. It sounds like *China tea*, so I imagine a cup of China tea—using taste this time.

OK, move on. *Caribbean Sea*. Imagine a picture of a Caribbean island. Maybe it's somewhere you wish you were now. Perhaps you've been there on vacation. What size is it? Actually fix it to the location. Is it hanging up on a wall? If there's no wall, maybe you're outside in the town; maybe it's on the ground.

Move on. We're nearly there. *Mediterranean Sea*. *Med*—all you need is a little mental trigger. I imagine seeing a *medal*. That will help me remember *Mediterranean*, so *medal*. What sort of medal is it? Is it shiny? Fix that to the location.

Next stage: *Bering Sea*. Bering. What do you associate the word *Bering* with? How about *ball bearings*? Maybe you walk on some ball bearings that you didn't know were there, and you slipped up.

Now go to the final stage, the *Bay of Bengal*. Are you thinking of a Bengal tiger? That's a pretty colorful character.

Great.

Now all the work has been done by your imagination. You've used association, and hopefully the journey has preserved the order of the information that you've just visualized. If you've used those three ingredients, there's a good chance that you can repeat the order of those oceans and seas. Let's see.

Don't rush into this. Just go back to the first stage, and what do you see? I'll help you a little bit. Remember I suggested using a *pack* of cards? What does that trigger? *Pacific Ocean*. Good.

Go to the next stage. Now what do you see? An atlas? An *atlas* triggers Atlantic Ocean. Are you getting the hang of this now?

Go to the third stage. What do you see there? You bumped into an *Indian*, a Cherokee, so it's *Indian Ocean*.

Next stage. Are you walking underneath something? What shape is it? An *arch*? So it's *Arctic Ocean*. Good.

Next stage. You meet an *Arabian knight*, so *Arabian Sea*. This time imagine that he has the number 5 attached to him. This is to help you remember that this is the fifth stage of the journey. Good; leave him alone.

Next stage. This is the clue: you're tasting something. *China tea*: *South China Sea*.

Next stage is a picture of an *island*. Whereabouts is it? It's in the *Caribbean Sea*.

Moving on. Something shiny. That's it: a *medal*. *Mediterranean Sea*.

Now move on to the next stage. Do you trip up here on some *ball bearings*? So it's *Bering Sea*.

Finally, there's a big, colorful *Bengal* tiger, so *Bengal Sea*.

Now if you go back again, you should be able to fly through those oceans and seas. As you do this, it's like creating pathways which get wider and wider the more you walk through them. After a while, you'll just be able to float through the list and go *Pacific Ocean*, *Atlantic Ocean*, *Indian Ocean*, *Arctic Ocean*, *Arabian Sea*, and so on. Now you can pinpoint any one of those objects. If I say, "What's the fifth sea on that list?" You think back. Oh. yes, we attached the number 5, to the *Arabian knight*, didn't we? Now you can tell me what the fourth item on the list is. Just go back one stage on the journey. It has to be the *arch*, which represents *Arctic Ocean*.

What takes an age for me to describe can be worked out by your brain in seconds. Again, the more you practice this method, the faster you'll get at it. Probably you're already beginning to notice that you're getting more creative. Maybe even it's a bit of a strain on your brain. That's a good sign. What's the old saying? "If it's not hurting, it's not working."

On the practical side, just think what you could do with this method. You could memorize any-thing: a grocery list, a list of names, things you have to do throughout the day. It's endless, and the more you practice this technique, the better you'll get at it.

Play around with the journey method. It's your challenge to your friends and your family. Just see how far you can take it.

In the next chapter, I'm going to give you the solution to the number one memory complaint: how to remember names and faces. With this technique, which is really powerful, you'll never forget a name again.

6

Never Forget Another Name or Face

Once, at a dinner party in London's fashionable Mayfair district, I was once asked to recall the names of everybody present. There were 100 people at this party, and the hostess asked me to memorize the first name and the surname of each guest. She said, "Look, I'm not going to say who you are. I just want you to go around and memorize everybody." I had never met any of them before.

A wealthy businessman to my right, who didn't know I was a memory man, thought this impossible. He said, "If you can do that, I'll give you £50,000 to gamble with in Las Vegas."

So I went around, discreetly got hold of one person from each table, and asked, "Could you just feed me the first name and surname of each person at this table?" They did. I managed to do this in about 20 or 25 minutes.

I got back to the table, and the businessman said, "Do you have that?"

"Yes, I think so," I said.

Rather nervously, he said, "Right. Well, you'd better start recording everybody before you forget them."

"No," I said, "I'm feeling a bit hungry. I'll wait until they're on their coffee." Sure enough, when the coffee came around, I stood up and named everybody perfectly, much to the surprise of the hostess and to the dismay of the businessman (which reminds me: we've still yet to fix a date to go to Las Vegas).

Before I trained my memory, I could never have done this. A few years ago, memorizing 100 people at a party would have been impossible. Like most people, I used to have a lot of difficulty remembering names and faces.

People regularly come up to me and say, "I'm very good at remembering faces, but I just can't remember the names." Why is it so difficult to remember names? I think one difficulty is that we're meeting more and more people. There's a wider name base. We have to confront new, alien names. We're living in a cosmopolitan society, so we get exotic, unusual sounds, like Boutros Boutros-Ghali (the late secretary general of the United Nations). They're very difficult and tricky to cope with.

Back in the old days, things were a lot easier. We had names like Smith, Baker, Butcher, so we identified somebody or connected them with their trade: Sawyer, Cooper. We'd have things like Harry the Baker, Tom the Fletcher. We knew by direct association. There was a link between the name and the profession.

Now when we meet somebody, there's no direct link to go on. What is a Ted, a Bob, a Julia, Carol supposed to look like in the first place? I mean, I no more look like Dominic than you look like your name, so don't feel guilty that you can't remember names easily. There is no name or face recollection system in the brain.

ALWAYS GIVE A FACE A PLACE

If there's no obvious link, then we have to create one. The English author Sir Thomas Browne said, "It is the common wonder of all men how amongst so many millions there should be none alike." Of so many millions of faces, not one is alike. We are all unique, and that's something we can use.

Just to recap: we used a journey to remember a shopping list of 10 items. We used association, location, and imagination. These are the three common denominators right throughout this course.

To remember a face, the phrase I have is, *always give a face a place.* I'm not going to bother about techniques when trying to remember a face. We're naturally very good at that. We've had to be over the centuries. We need to know at first judgment if somebody's going to be a friend or a foe. We can remember faces, but it's just getting the name to them. So, give a face a place.

Somebody comes up to you in the street and says, "Oh, hi, Donnie. How are you doing?" You know that face so well, but you can't remember who that person is. What are you trying to do? You're trying to place that person. Once you have that place, then all the information concerning that person will come back to you. "Hi. Don't you remember me? It's George. We met at that convention in London."

Ah, so now you have the place. "Yes, you're the guy that sells that crazy diet. How is the book coming along?" Once you know the label of the file, you know where to go and look it up.

Now I'm going to give you four techniques to help you remember names to help you give a face a place.

YOU REMIND ME OF SOMEONE

Here's technique number one, and it's called, "You Remind Me of Someone." Look at a face and think if they resemble anybody, even vaguely, like a friend or a musician. Maybe they look like somebody royal, a sportsperson, or a politician. Try to make the connection fairly immediate.

Say you meet somebody; maybe she has a strange mannerism. She reminds you of your aunt. Now you have a first vital link. Your aunt gives you a location—your aunt's house—so this is the chain of associations. This is exactly how memory works. We're looking for something to grab hold of. That person reminds you of your aunt, so now you think of your aunt's house.

Actually do this yourself. Think of your aunt, and think of her house. Now you need the name. The woman says her name is Mrs. Shepard. Simple. You just associate or imagine seeing a shepherd standing outside your aunt's house. Here's the complete chain: You have the look-alike stage; she looks like your aunt. That gives you a place, so that's the location: your aunt's house. Now you put in the key image, which is a shepherd. So you've gone *face*, *location*, *key image*.

Let's take another case. Suppose somebody reminds you of the character J. R. Ewing in *Dal-*

las. What location could you use? You could use Southfork Ranch from the series. The man comes out with a name: it's Mr. Walski. Now you imagine this person at Southfork Ranch skiing up one of the walls. That's a really crazy image, but it's memorable. Again, this is the link: you have *face*, *place*, and the *key image*, where you've created a scene.

WHAT'S MY LINE?

Now we move onto technique number two. This is called "What's My Line?" If the person doesn't look like anybody familiar or famous, then think what sort of work this person does. What's their line of business? (I've always been told, don't judge a book by its cover, and you shouldn't pigeonhole people, but you can't help doing it, can you?)

You look at somebody for the first time, and you think that person looks a bit like a lawyer, a journalist, a musician, or maybe your doctor or a tax collector. It doesn't matter what it is; what we're looking for here is a place.

Let's take an example. For whatever reason, you meet somebody who looks like a typical car salesman. Now think of your own garage. A car salesman makes you think of a car showroom, so think of your own garage or a local car showroom. Now you wait for the name. We'll do the first name this time.

The man says his name is George. The trick here is to use somebody else that you already know called George. It might be a friend of yours or an uncle. How about George Bush? So you imagine: George Bush at the showroom, trying to sell a car.

Now you wait for the surname. The surname is Baker. Again, we make an associated image. Imagine George Bush with a baker's hat on. This is the chain: *profession*, *place*, *key image*.

The beauty of this method is that it works both ways.

If you're at a party, and you meet a crowd of people, and you use these techniques, when you hear the name *Baker*, you'll think, "Wait a minute. Who was that? Oh, yes. It was the baker's hat on George Bush, and he was standing at the car show-room. It must be that guy over there." It's the use of those three ingredients again: association, imagination, location.

Let's take another case. Supposing you meet somebody who looks like a typical tax inspector. In this case, you would use the location of your tax office. So think about your tax office, where it is situated. Use that as a mental backdrop. You wait for the name.

The man's name is Mr. Overton. Again, what's the first thing that comes into your head? Maybe you think of putting a ton weight over his head. (By the way, you should never tell people how you remember their names. It can lead to all sorts of insults and arguments.) So you have the image of putting a ton weight over the man's head at the tax office.

THE FEATURE LINK

What if a face has no look-alike, and a place doesn't come to mind, like job surroundings? The idea then is to create an artificial link. If the face doesn't take you to a place, then we get on to technique number three. This is called the *feature link*.

Maybe somebody has some interesting features, maybe a pointed nose or outsized earrings, or distinguishing marks of some sort. Maybe they have a tattoo or an interesting trait. All you're looking for is something to latch onto.

For example, you're introduced to a woman called Pat Whitehead. You notice that she has streaks of white hair. I know it's an obvious link, but just imagine patting her on the head. Maybe she's had some paint poured over her, and your hands are covered with white paint. It doesn't really matter how you get there, as long as you make that connection, so the next time you see her you think, "Oh, yes, streaks of paint, white. Oh, yes, white head," and you've patted her. "Pat Whitehead."

In this case, the person's actual physique has become the location in itself. So this is the link: it's gone *person, feature, scene.*

Again, never tell anybody how you've gotten to remember their name. Just say you have a good memory. I once made a mistake at a meeting. A guy said, "How did you remember my name?"

"Well," I said, "you have rather pointed ears, so I thought of Dr. Spock from *Star Trek.* So I visualized you on the deck of the Starship *Enterprise.*" He walked off in disgust. From then onwards, I learned to keep my thoughts to myself.

This particular technique is a favorite amongst stage performers and magicians, and they probably wouldn't thank me for revealing it to you. They look out for particular types of clothing so they can attach or link the name in some crazy image to that particular clothing. The only trouble with this is clothes change, but faces don't.

FIRST NAME PLACES

All three of the above methods are good, but now I'm going to tell you the most powerful one. I've used it to remember audiences of anything up to 300 people in one go. I did this once on *Oprah* a couple of years back. I call technique number four "First Name Places." This is how I do it.

The first thing I want to know is the person's first name. That's my first hook, the first link in the chain. That name will transport that person to a specific location somewhere in the world. If I go up to the first person in the audience and say, "Give me your first name," she says, "Carol." Immediately I think of a specific church in England. Why *Carol*? *Carol* makes me think of *carol* singing, and that's something that I do every Christmas. So I go to that same church as soon as I hear the name *Carol*. Now I have a place.

If she had said her name was Jean, then I would go straight to a jean shop in my hometown of Guildford. Why? Because that's where I bought my first pair of jeans. If the name is Pamela, then I go to my mother's house, because my mother's name is Pamela. If it's George, then I go to the White House. If it's Larry, I think of Larry King, so I use the news desk at CNN, and I base the mnemonic scene that I'm going to create around CNN.

Let's go through an example together. Let's say the first person that I meet is called Leo. Immediately I go straight to the *Titanic*. Can you think of why? Leonardo DiCaprio. It doesn't matter if that person doesn't look like Leonardo DiCaprio. It's just the name that I'm using to transport that face to the location. So now I sort of energize that person *Star Trek* style. He's now going off to the *Titanic*.

Now I ask for the surname. Leo's surname is *Taylor*. What do I do? I imagine that person onboard the *Titanic* with a tape measure around his neck. That's all I need. When I go back to that person, I think, "Ah, yes. I sent you off to the *Titanic*. You have a tape measure around your neck. It has to be Leo Taylor." Highly unlikely, surreal image, but I don't care. I can remember his name, and I do that methodically with each person. I have a solid chain of links.

How do I remember 100 names in an audience? I have a whole dossier of places that I can send people to. If I hear the name *Terry*, I think of a friend's house, because he's a decorator, so that person then goes to Terry's house in England. If I hear the name *Nicola*, I can't help thinking of a specific wine bar where I dated a girl called Nicola. The date was unsuccessful, but I don't care. I can still remember it.

REMEMBERING MORE COMPLICATED NAMES

"OK," I hear you say, "but what if you have a more challenging name, something with 2, 3, or 4 syllables or more?"

All you have to do is break the name down into syllables and make more complex scenes.

For instance, the name *Radwandski*, now I would break that down into *rad*, *wand*, and *ski*. *Rad* makes me think of *radiator*, *wand* a magic *wand*, and *ski* a *ski*, of course. Where there's a will, there's a way. You can break any name down into syllables and consequently into pictures.

Take the name *Dougherty*. I think of *docker's tea break*. *Hathaway* makes me think of *hats away*. How about *Jameson*? *Jamey in the sun*. *Oppenheimer*, *open home*. *Rachmaninoff*: you can have *rack*, *man*, in *oven*. The match doesn't have to be exact. You're just looking for a trigger. How about *Neacher*? I think of *knee itcher*.

What if two people double up? Supposing I meet somebody else in the audience called Leo. No problem at all. All I do is transport that person to a different part of the ship. If there are three or four Leos, then they just mix around the helm of the ship, or they may be in a life raft or somewhere else. In fact, it even helps, because I can group them all together.

What about 300 people? It doesn't just happen. I don't suddenly absorb all the information from 300 people. I have to work methodically, one at a time. It takes a bit longer, but I can guarantee I have them all in my head. I transport 300 people off to different parts of the world. Try it. It really does work.

To recap: give a face a place. Study a face, and just think whom they remind you of. Take the nearest look-alike. They might look like John McEnroe, an archvillain, an actor, hero, or maybe a relative or friend. Just allow resemblance to take them to a place. If somebody looks like Tiger Woods, then base the scene around Augusta. Use colorful, imaginative scenes to remember the name.

What if they don't have a look-alike? Use "What's My Line?" Where would you expect that person to work? Look at the person and see what sort of job they'd be likely to have—like a law enforcement officer or a bank clerk or a hairdresser. Use their place of work to provide a mental backdrop.

What if that person doesn't take you anywhere? What if that person doesn't have a look-alike, or you can't think what job they might have? In that case, you would use a feature link. Maybe they're called *Pearson*, so they have *piercing eyes*. Or they're *Cooper*, so you imagine them being *barrel-shaped*.

I think the most powerful method is first-name places. Let the first name transport that person to a place. If the name is Dennis, you could take him to the dentist. If the name is Zoe, she can go to a zoo.

A FIRST-NAME EXERCISE

Here's an exercise for you. I'm going to list a series of first names. As soon as you read each name, I want you to immediately associate that name with a specific location. It doesn't really matter how or why you arrive at that location. Your brain is so used to making connections that it's sometimes difficult to keep pace with your own chain of thoughts.

If I say the name *Lisa*, you might immediately think of an art museum. Why? Even if you don't realize it, *Lisa* could make you think of the famous *Mona Lisa* and da Vinci. Hence, the art museum. If I say the name *Bernard*, you might be thinking of Switzerland and a St. Bernard dog, or the name *Barbara* might make you think of Barbra Streisand on location for a film.

I'm going to feed you a series of names, and let that particular name suggest a place. This is personal to you. Try to get an associated place immediately, as soon as you read the name.

Michael	Richard
Karen	Elizabeth
Peter	George
James	Mary
Caroline	Bobby

Did you notice that as soon as you heard the name, you were able to think of an associated place? That's a very useful mechanism to have, because we can use it to store massive amounts of information about each person. That's the mechanism of association, and that's how it can work for you.

This time, I'm going to list the same first names again, but I'm going to add surnames. Now, when you hear the name *Michael*, I want you to create a little image based on the surname and fix it to that mental backdrop.

Michael Stamp	Richard Glass
Karen Barber	Elizabeth Fox
Peter Baker	George Ford
James Neacher	Mary Nightingale
Caroline Taylor	Bobby Kowalski

We're looking for immediate associations here. Let me pick one of those surnames at random, and see if you can remember the first name. If I say *Taylor*, what are you thinking of? Whom are you connecting that to? It should be *Caroline*.

Let's make it slightly easier. Let's do the first name first. If I say *Michael*, you should be at a location now, and you should have fixed an image of *Stamp*. Let's give you another first name. How about *Mary*? What are you thinking of now? Can you see a bird there? *Mary Nightingale*.

I'm going to give you another surname: *Fox*. Where was the fox? Wherever the location is, that should trigger the first name, which is *Elizabeth*. *Bobby*—what place were you thinking of when I said *Bobby*? You had a pretty difficult name: *Kowalski*. Here are all those names again.

Michael Stamp	Richard Glass
Karen Barber	Elizabeth Fox
Peter Baker	George Ford
James Neacher	Mary Nightingale
Caroline Taylor	Bobby Kowalski

How many of those did you get? I tried this test on a friend of mine recently, and she said she got 8 out of 10, but she had a lot of trouble with Peter Baker and James Neacher.

"Why is that?" I said.

"I'm glad those people are out of my life—Peter and James. That's why I had trouble. I didn't really want to think about them."

Here's what I suggest you do. It's quite difficult to begin with, because you're using your brain in a different way. Just as practice, I suggest you flip through a magazine or a newspaper. You always get unfamiliar faces there, and they normally put the names just underneath. Try applying the techniques to see how many of those names you can remember. You could do a competition with your family or friends and see how many you can remember.

The next time you're at a party, try it out. It's a great party trick as well as a great exercise. If you really get confident, why don't you use it in the work environment? It's a great way of meeting new people.

In effect, it's like carrying a 3D internal filing cabinet. You have a file on everybody. Once you have a location for each person, then you just keep adding more and more images. If you remember, in the example I gave you, Leo Taylor was onboard ship on the *Titanic*. If you want to build up more information about him, just keep adding more images. Maybe you can store his wife's name or the fact that he likes going skiing or that he drives a Chevrolet. Just stick the Chevrolet onboard the ship.

People are going to start asking, "How do you remember all this stuff? Where is this guy getting his information from?" You're using this internal mental filing cabinet, which is full of names. Don't tell them. Just say you have a good memory.

It's embarrassing to forget people's names. It's one of the biggest insults to forget somebody after a short time (like 30 seconds after you've met them). Remembering their name is also one of the biggest compliments you can pay somebody, particularly if you haven't seen them for a long time. How to win friends and influence people? Remember their names.

In the next chapter, we're going to work more on names and faces, and I'm going to give you another exercise. Until then, keep practicing the techniques that you've learned up to this point.

7

Dominic Plays "Trivial Pursuit"

. . . .

A few years ago, I did a promotion for the game "Trivial Pursuit." I had to spend a few weeks memorizing a total of 7,500 questions and answers. As part of the promotion, I was asked to appear at a famous toy shop called Hamleys on Regent Street in London. There was an ad in the paper beforehand, which said, "Challenge the memory man. If he gets a question wrong, you win £50. If he gets two questions wrong, then you win £100. If he gets a third question wrong, then you win £5,000."

When I arrived at Hamleys, there was a huge queue stretching all the way down Regent Street. Anyway, I got to the top of the building. I had a briefcase with me. I put it down, they dropped the rope, and everybody ran towards the front of the queue.

After about 10 minutes or so, things were going well—I got all the questions right—but I noticed somebody in the queue. He kept leaning forward and looking around. He looked a bit shifty as well. I don't know if you ever get that feeling that something's going to go wrong. Well, I sensed it with this particular guy.

Sure enough, when he got to the head of the queue and it was his turn, he said, "Before I ask a question of Mr. O'Brien, I want that briefcase removed."

"Absolutely, no problem," I said. "Move it wherever you like."

"Send it to the back of the room." A couple of guys came along and moved it to the back of the room.

He said, "No, I want it further away. I want it out of earshot."

Somehow this guy thought that I was cheating. Maybe I had a little man or a speaker inside or something.

Anyway, once the man was satisfied that the briefcase was far enough away, he came out with a question: "How old was Anna Kournikova in May 1992, when she was described as the finest tennis prospect of the century?"

I said, "Ten."

He threw the card down and said, "Oh, this is a fiddle," and walked off. Well, it wasn't a fiddle. I was able to come up with the answer because I was thinking of Dudley Moore. Why Dudley Moore? He was in the film *10*.

All I needed from that question were two words: *Anna* and *tennis*. Anna made me think of a friend's house, and she plays tennis. I know she has a tennis court. Then I just imagined Dudley Moore playing tennis there, and the answer was simple. I was using mnemonics.

WHAT ARE MNEMONICS?

Put simply, a mnemonic is any device that aids memory. An acronym is a mnemonic. Probably the most famous acronym for British schoolchildren is "Richard of York goes battling in vain." That gives you the colors in their order in the spectrum: red, orange, yellow, green, blue, indigo, violet. If you take the first letter from each word, it gives you ROYGBIV. Of course, you could just think of the name "Roy G. Biv."

Now we'll learn how to use mnemonics to translate numbers into colorful, meaningful, and of course memorable images. I call this the language of numbers. Later I'll explain a system that

I developed which I believe has been pivotal in enabling me to win the World Memory Championships for a record eight times. This system is so devastatingly effective that unfortunately for me, my rivals are now using it to try to beat me, and one or two are getting rather too close for comfort. I've christened it the Dominic system, but more of that later.

For now, to ease you into the language of numbers, we're going to look at a couple of standard methods of translating single-digit numbers into mnemonic symbols. They're very easy to learn, and they can be very useful for remembering a whole host of numerical data, like your bank PIN number or any other short sequence of numbers.

What's a number shape? Well, the clue is in the title. Number shape. The idea is to associate—there's that word *association* again—a single number with its nearest everyday look-alike shape.

For example, the number 5 has the shape of a curtain hook. The number 6 looks like the shape of an elephant's trunk. The number 8 looks like a snowman or maybe an hourglass. What about the number 2? Does that look a little bit like a swan?

In this case, the swan becomes the key image for the number 2. We're going to be using a lot of key images in this course. How about the number 1? That looks like a pencil or maybe a candle.

By the way, you can do what you like in the privacy of your own mind. If you think that number looks like the shape of a phallic symbol, well, then, use it. One word of warning: don't explain to other people how you can remember certain numbers.

I'm going to give you a number, and then I'm going to give you its associated number shape. Here goes:

    1: candle
    2: swan
    3: handcuffs
    4: sailboat
    5: curtain hook
    6: elephant's trunk
    7: boomerang
    8: snowman
    9: balloon and string
   10: stick and hoop

Of course you can choose your own number shapes. For number 10, for instance, why don't you have Laurel and Hardy? For number 8, you can use Marilyn Monroe. Whatever comes to mind, you could even have a number shape for the number 0. I think 0 looks like a football.

How can we put this in practical use? Well, for instance, the planet Mars has 2 moons. To remember that fact, you might imagine a swan gracefully flapping its wings as it endlessly orbits Mars. Remember, the number shape for 2 is a swan.

AN EXERCISE

Do you have all of the number shapes in your head? Let's have a quick test. What's the association for number 7? Boomerang. 9? Balloon and string. How about the number 1? Candle.

If you think you're ready to go, let's try a little exercise. I'm going to give you a question, and I'm also going to give you the answer. Somehow you have to connect them by using all those three ingredients: imagination, association, and of course location. For example, to remember that Adam and Eve had 3 children, imagine them being handcuffed: handcuffs is the number shape for 3. When you're ready, here goes.

How many hundred rooms does Buckingham Palace have? The answer is 6. How are you going to connect an elephant's trunk to that question?

Next one: how many horses are there on a polo team? Answer: 4. Remember the number shape for 4 is a sailboat. You make the association.

How many reindeer pull Santa's sleigh? That should be an easy one, because the number shape for 8, which is the answer, is a snowman.

What magic number helped bring down the walls of Jericho? Answer; 7.

How many teats does a female goat have? The answer: 2, or a swan.

The Titanic went down with how many funnels? The answer: 4. Again, you have a ready-made image for that.

How many children did Adam and Eve have? You already know the answer. Handcuffs, which gives you 3.

How many wings does a bee have? Answer: 4.

How many petals does a wild English rose have? The answer to that is 5. Remember the number shape for 5 is a curtain hook.

Good. Now, assuming that you've employed a combination of imagination, association and location, you should be able to answer these questions.

Adam and Eve had how many children? Think of the handcuffs: 3.

Buckingham Palace has how many hundred rooms? What was the association there? Elephant's trunk, so it has to be 600 rooms.

What magic number helped bring down the walls of Jericho? Clue: boomerang. So the answer is 7.

How many teats does a female goat have? Think about it. What was your number shape? Swan? The answer is 2.

The *Titanic* went down with how many funnels? Well, the number shape for 4 is a sailboat, so you had a ready-made association there.

How many wings does a bee have? Answer: 4.

How many petals does a wild English Rose have? Answer: 5. That was the curtain hook.

How many horses are there on a polo team? Think about the number shape. Sailboat: it has to be 4.

Finally, how many reindeer pulled Santa's sleigh? That's an easy one, because it's the number shape of a snowman, which is 8.

You might want to go back and test yourself tomorrow or in a week's time. If the mental pictures you created were sufficiently stimulating, you may find that you're stuck with this information permanently.

THE NUMBER RHYME SYSTEM

More about number shapes later. The second system is called the *number rhyme system*. Again, the clue is in the description. The idea is to associate the number with its nearest rhyming word. Let's give you some examples.

You would associate the number 4 with *door* or *sore*; 7 you'd connect with *heaven* or *Kevin*. How about 6? You could connect that with *sticks* or *bricks*.

I'm going to go through the list now from 1 to 10, and I'm going to give you a suggestion for a number rhyme. Of course, you can use your own.

1: gun
2: shoe
3: tree
4: door
5: hive
6: sticks
7: heaven
8: gate
9: wine
10: pen

Got those? Now we're going to do a little game. I'm going to get you to memorize the last 10 presidents of the 20th century, so make sure you have the number rhyme system clearly in your head.

Do you have that? Quick test. What's the rhyme for 8? Gate. What's the key image for 9? Wine. How about 2? Shoe, and 6 is stick; 1, gun; 4, door, 5, hive. If you've got those right, then we'll progress with the exercise.

I'm going to list the 10 presidents in order, starting with Truman. He's number 1, and somehow you have to connect its key image, in this case *gun*, which rhymes with 1, with *Truman*. When I say the number 7, and the number rhyme is *heaven*, I will list *Carter*. Now he's a bit of a saint; he's going to go straight to heaven, isn't he? You connect *Carter* with *heaven*, so you know he's the seventh president. Here we go:

1: gun, Truman
2: shoe, Eisenhower
3: tree, Kennedy
4: door, Johnson
5: hive, Nixon
6: sticks, Ford
7: heaven, Carter
8: gate, Reagan
9: wine, Bush
10: pen, Clinton

Keep thinking all the time. This time I'm just going to list the number, and I want you to write down the president.

1	6
2	7
3	8
4	9
5	10

How many did you get? Did you get all 10? I wonder what was going through your mind with some of these. How would you connect, for instance, *Kennedy* to *tree*, or *Clinton* with *pen*? What would Bill Clinton be doing with a pen? Maybe rewriting the past.

You can do lots of things with this. You can pinpoint any one of those presidents. If I say 5, that makes you think of *hive*, which you connect with Nixon. You could go forward. You could go from Truman right the way through Clinton. You could go backwards as well. You can do it in reverse.

If I say to you, "Bush," you can tell me what number on the list he is. Bush makes you think of what? *Wine*, which gives you 9. What would Eisenhower be? You think of *shoe*, which gives you the number 2.

Can you see how the pieces of the memory puzzle are beginning to fit together like pieces of a jigsaw puzzle? That's because you're using your imagination as well as association and location.

SOME PRACTICAL USES

You want to practice these systems. Use the number shapes or the number rhymes, whichever you prefer, but they're very useful for memorizing all sorts of information.

How can we use this on a more practical level? Well, you could use it to memorize your bank PIN number.

For example, let's say your number is 4135. Just translate those into key images using the number rhyme system. So you have 4, door; 1, gun; 3, tree; 5, hive. What do you think the right location would be to store your bank PIN number? Well, think of your bank. Just imagine your bank, and how would you fit a little miniepic around your bank using *door*, *gun*, *tree*, and *hive*?

Imagine the door bursting open, and there's somebody there with a gun, and he runs up a tree, only to find there's a beehive up there. All you have to do is think about that again, and you have the bank PIN number for as long as you want. Door, 4; gun, 1; tree, 3; hive, 5. Of course, after a while, you'll build up a verbal recall of the number, but isn't it nice to have a backup just in case verbal recall lets you down?

If you really want to get into numbers, in the next chapter we're going to get serious. I'm talking telephone numbers, big ones, like thousands. Until then, use the techniques that I've described here. Use number shapes and number rhymes to help you remember any sort of number. Then you'll really find that you're developing your own quantum memory power.

8

The Dominic System

Have you ever seen a memory performer on television reciting a long number? Maybe you've seen me on television, or maybe you've read about these guys who can remember telephone directories. What about the character in from *Rain Man* who could remember the order of sticks on the floor? He did a telephone directory and cards and numbers.

You're probably wondering how this is possible. As I mentioned, in 2018 I was able to remember 1,780 digits—that's a random sequence of digits—in just about 60 minutes. How is this possible?

Originally I designed this system to allow me to memorize gigantic numbers. I used this to break records and win World Memory Championships, but somewhere along the line when I was developing this system, I began to realize that you could use it to remember a whole range of things—telephone numbers, appointments, statistics, equations, birthdays, and if you're a student, maybe atomic weights, atomic numbers, history dates—anything involving a number.

If you think about it, why is it so easy to remember faces and pictures, but for some reason when it comes to numbers, we're stumped? Our brains have something like 86 billion neurons. We're very clever people, and yet our memory span for numbers is about 6 or 7 digits.

It seems a bit unfair, because we live in a world of numbers, and without them, life would be chaotic. Take telephone bills, gas bills, appointments, exam results, train timetables, weights, measures, bank statistics, account numbers. We live in a world of numbers. Everything has to be tallied, quantified, and reckoned. Numbers count.

Now if I give you a number, let's say 34286492, it doesn't register, does it? You probably forget it immediately. But say I have some good news for you: you've won the lottery. You've won a record $34,286,492. Doesn't that number all of a sudden have some resonance? It means something.

We can really only understand numbers if they have some significance. Otherwise they're unintel-

ligible, inanimate, monotonous. They're positively
dull and forgettable, because they don't have any
character.

Now you're asking yourself, how can this guy
memorize 1,780 digits? The reason is that I actually
give numbers a character. I breathe life into them,
and this is the heart of a system I have christened
the *Dominic system*. If you're one for acronyms,
you can call it the *Decipherment of Mnemonically
Interpreted Numbers into Characters*.

When I see a pair of numbers, I don't just see
numbers. I see a person. For example, when I see
the number 10, I see Dudley Moore. Why Dudley
Moore? Because he was in the film *10*. When I see
the number 23, I think of Bing Crosby. Why Bing
Crosby? If you take the second and third letters of
the alphabet, that gives you B and C, Bing Crosby's initials.

Let's give you another one. If I see the number 07, what do you think of? I think of James
Bond. Another one: 72; I think of George Bush.
Why George Bush? Well, the seventh letter of the
alphabet is G, and the second is B: George Bush's
initials. For every pair of numbers from 00 to 99, I
see a person.

Furthermore, each character, each personal-
ity has their own unique prop and action. In Bing
Crosby's case, number 23, I have him decorating a

Christmas tree, because I keep thinking of the film
White Christmas. James Bond is wearing a white
tuxedo, and he's carrying a gun. I associate Dudley
Moore with playing the piano, because he's a great
pianist.

I have a code that will enable you to translate
numbers into people. It's just 10 numbers trans-
lated into letters.

1 = A	6 = S
2 = B	7 = G
3 = C	8 = H
4 = D	9 = N
5 = E	0 = O

Number 1 is A. That's the first letter of the
alphabet; 2 is B; 3 is C; 4 is D; Five is E. For 6,
there's a slight change here. It's an S, because it
has a sort of a sexy sound. Now we go back to
normal. Seven is G. H is 8. Nine, that's an N. Zero
looks like the letter O, so it's an O.

Once you have those letters in your head and
you know how to translate them, you can get all
sorts of combinations of initials for people. Take
the number 33: that translates into CC. Now you
have Charlie Chaplin. How about the number 43?
That gives you DC. How about David Copperfield,
the magician?

Over the next few days or weeks, using the table below as a sample, start to associate pairs of numbers with people. This could be a whole range of people: royalty, politicians, family, friends. You could also have fictitious characters.

Numbers	Letters	Person	Action
00	OO	Olive Oyl	Eating spinach
06	OS	Omar Sharif	Playing bridge
07	OG	Organ grinder	Holding monkey
08	OH	Oliver Hardy	Berating Stan
09	ON	Oliver North	In denial

It's a deeply personal thing. For instance, the number 57 is a friend of the family called Theresa. When I was born, Theresa came along and helped my mother to raise the family. Why 57? That's the year I was born. I always associate Theresa with 57. Let's say for the number 49, you might have a favorite sports person from the 49ers, so this is where it starts to get fun. Apart from everything else, it's a great exercise for the brain.

If you can't find a direct association between a number and a person, then use the code I gave above. You can decode the numbers into letters. For instance, 53 to me is Eric Clapton, EC, because E is the fifth letter of the alphabet and C is the third. As I mentioned, each figure should have a prop and an action, so Eric Clapton is playing the guitar.

Why do I have every pair of numbers as a person and not an object? As I said before, I've developed these techniques and systems over time. I've thrown out the techniques that didn't work. Originally, each pair of numbers used to be an object, so the number 35 would be a book. The number 47 was a vase, for some reason, and 19 an umbrella. But I was finding these difficult to remember when I was trying to memorize long sequences of numbers.

Then I threw in the odd person. I found that it was far easier to remember the people than it was to remember the objects, because objects tend to be dull as well. You can shout until you're blue in the face at a vase, and it won't flinch. If you shout at a person, they're liable to shout back, and they might even throw a vase at you. People are versatile, flexible. You can put them into any circumstance, any location. That's the key. So let's have some more examples, and remember, we need to put props and actions into this process.

Take the number 08. That translates into *Oliver Hardy*, O and H. His action is swinging a plank. How about the original comedian, Charlie Chaplin, number 33? His action is bending a cane. What about the number 18, 1-8? To me, that's *Alfred*

Hitchcock. I always associate him with the film *Psycho*, so I have him taking a shower.

PRACTICAL USES

How can we put this to practical use? I want you now to imagine your train station. I'm going to give you a time. This is the time the train leaves on the hour, every hour. Picture your own train station. The train leaves at eight minutes past every hour. Imagine the platform with Oliver Hardy swinging his plank and maybe causing chaos, knocking all the passengers onto the railway track. OK, got that image?

Here's another one. Suppose there's a friend of yours arriving at the bus station. The first thing is you have to go to the location. Remember those three key ingredients: association, location, imagination. Think of your own bus station. Your friend is arriving on the number 53 bus, which translates to Eric Clapton. So have Eric driving the bus. Maybe he's singing, "You Look Wonderful Tonight."

It could be a little more complicated. Suppose the number of the bus is 532. This is where you have to get a bit inventive.

Remember the number shapes. We can have a pair of numbers, 53, which is Eric, followed by the number shape for 2, which is a swan. So imagine

Eric on the bus holding a swan. A bizarre image, but a memorable one. Now you'll remember the number of the bus: 532.

Or you have a client, and he's asked you to phone him back. His extension number is 184. How are you going to remember that? The first thing you ought to do is think of the location. Think of his office.

Now we break the number into a person and a number shape. So 18 is Alfred Hitchcock. He's at your friend's office, and what's the number shape for 4? It's a sailboat. Picture Alfred Hitchcock in a sailboat, and this is happening in your friend's office. So, you're connecting, you're anchoring this image and therefore the piece of information to that specific location.

A BIT MORE FUN

OK, let's make it a little bit more fun. Let's get on to 4-digit numbers now. Let's take the number 3135. This time we break that into pairs of numbers. So 3135 relates to Charles Atlas: 31, CA. and 35 relates to Clint Eastwood: CE. Charles Atlas's action is weightlifting; he's a bodybuilder. Clint Eastwood you would imagine smoking a cigar and saying, "Make my day, punk." How do we combine them?

If the number is 3135, you could have Charles Atlas using Clint's action, which is smoking a cigar. You could imagine Charles with a cigar in his mouth saying, "Make my day, punk."

What would happen if it was the other way around? Supposing it was 3531. What would you have then? Think about it. It would be Clint Eastwood bodybuilding or weightlifting.

Here's another example. The number 27 translates to BG. I think of the Bee Gees, and I associate them with wearing tight, white flares with one arm in the air, and singing "Night Fever." (If I tried to get in a pair of flares these days, I'd be impotent in two minutes flat, but that's the image.)

If you take the number 7227, that relates to 2 sets of people. George Bush is 72, GB, and 27 is the Bee Gees. Now, can you see where I'm coming from here? George Bush is going to take on the Bee Gees' action. You picture George Bush wearing tight white flares, one arm in the arm, singing "Night Fever."

This is where it starts to get fun. Let's take another 4-digit number. How about 3615? Well, 36 is, to me, Claudia Schiffer, 36, CS, and 15 is Albert Einstein, AE. I associate Claudia Schiffer with walking on a catwalk, Albert Einstein with chalking a formula on a blackboard. If you had 3615, it would be Claudia Schiffer chalking a formula on a blackboard.

What would you have with 1527? You'd have Albert Einstein singing "Night Fever." Or you could have 7236: George Bush striding up and down a catwalk. If you're keen on sports, to you 72 wouldn't be George Bush. It could be William "Refrigerator" Perry from the Chicago Bears, because he wore jersey number 72. Imagine him wearing tight, white flares singing "Night Fever." Instead of Bing Crosby for 23, you could have Michael Jordan, the basketball player, because he wears shirt number 23.

As you can see, you can use these characters to remember a whole range of numerical information. Can you see how suddenly you've breathed life into the numbers? They're animated, they're colorful.

Apart from anything else, this is an extremely beneficial exercise for the whole of your brain and for your creative imagination. Maybe thinking of all these details is beginning to strain your brain a little bit, but remember the adage, "If it's not hurting, it's not working," so keep at it.

APPOINTMENTS

Let's get on to appointments. Say you want to remember that you have an appointment with your dental hygienist on July 18. In this case, you would take the month, which would be 07, followed by

18. That gives you 2 characters again: 0–7, James Bond, and Alfred Hitchcock, 1–8.

What's the first thing you do? You think of the location, so think of the location of your dentist right now. Think of the place, the location. Got it?

Now it's up to you, how you devise your scene. It's going to be a miniepic. Maybe you could have James Bond chasing Alfred Hitchcock around the dental hygienist, or perhaps you go in there, and there's James Bond having a shower, which is Alfred Hitchcock's action.

Here's another for you. Let's say you bump into your lawyer in the street, and he says in a hurry, "Look, that court case has come up. It's November 23." You don't have a pen or paper on you, so how are you going to remember it? Just stay calm. Go through these techniques again step-by-step. What's the first thing you do?

Look at the subject of the conversation. It's court, so it has to be a courtroom. Now think of your own law courts. Do you have that? Now look at the date, November 23, and that translates into 1123. By this time, of course, you would have had an automatic association with people. Immediately I see tennis player Andre Agassi, which is 11, and 23 is Bing Crosby. So you could have Andre Agassi in the judge's seat, and maybe Bing Crosby is in the witness box.

It doesn't really matter how you get there, but now that you have that date turned into images, you will never forget it. Life is so much easier when you don't have to write things down.

ANOTHER JOURNEY EXERCISE

Before we get on to telephone numbers, I want to take you through an exercise. We did the journey through your house. I want you now extend that journey from your house out into the main road. A typical journey could start from your front door, for example. Then you go to your front gate, if you have one. The third stage could be the sidewalk. After that, maybe you have the bus stop. Perhaps you have a doughnut stand, and then finally, traffic lights. So this time, I just want 6 stages, so work that out.

Now that you have all 6 stages, we can lay down some more information. As always, the journey will preserve the order of the information that you're about to learn. We'll go through this one together. This time I'm going to give you a series of characters, so don't worry about the numbers for the time being. Just think about the characters.

Imagine that you're standing at the front door. You've just opened the door, and in front of you is Charles Atlas. Remember, he's the bodybuilder, so he's standing there lifting up a pair of weights.

Again, use all your cortical skills: touch, taste, sight, smell, sound. Use humor, exaggeration, color. Okay? Logic as well. What's he doing there? A bit of a shock, isn't it?

Now leave Charles alone. Go to the second stage of your journey. Maybe you're at the front gate. Whom do you meet there? This time you're going to meet Dan Aykroyd of *Ghostbusters* fame. What would you associate him with? Maybe he has that big power pack on, and he's shooting some ectoplasm, that slimy stuff. Got the picture there? A nice colorful picture.

You pass by Dan and go to the next stage. Maybe you're on the sidewalk. Make sure it's a nice, convenient stop. This time you're going to meet that famous character from the past, Emperor Nero. I see him with one hand sticking out, and he has his thumb down. He's giving you the thumb's down, for whatever reason. Look at him; now pass him by and go to the next stage of the journey. Maybe it's a bus stop. Wherever you are now, who's the next character? You're going to meet Bram Stoker, the author of *Dracula*. His action would be driving a stake in. This is happening at the fourth stage, wherever that is.

OK, just two more to go. At this point, you're at the fourth stage, which may be a doughnut stand. This time you're going to see Eric Clapton.

Obviously now you're going to use sound. He's playing his guitar. What sort of music is he playing? Is it an electric guitar? Acoustic? Maybe he's playing "Layla."

OK, say goodbye to Eric. Now go to the last stage, wherever that is. You may be at the traffic light now. This time you meet author Ernest Hemingway. I associate him with reading a book. Again, use your imaginative skills. Use a bit of exaggeration. Make the book a really big one, an outsized book, so it stands out in your mind.

Now we have 6 characters. Return and review the scenes in your mind. Don't rush into this. What happened at the front door? A guy with some weights. Yes, it's Charles Atlas. Now go to the front gate. Who is it? Somebody shooting ectoplasm. It has to be Dan Aykroyd.

OK, move on. Who can you see now? Emperor Nero, the guy with the thumbs down. Moving on, you see Bram Stoker driving a stake in. Second to last, we have somebody playing something. It has to be Eric Clapton playing the guitar. Finally is the guy with the book: Ernest Hemingway.

If you think about that, you could probably go backwards or forwards. Did you notice anything about those people? What I've done, whether you like it or not, is trick you into memorizing the first eleven places to pi. Pi is that infinite number, and

what you've just memorized by translating them
back into numbers is this: 3.1, that gives you
Charles Atlas, 31; 41 is Dan Aykroyd, DA; 59, EN,
Emperor Nero; 26. which is Bram Stoker; 53, Eric
Clapton; 58, Ernest Hemingway.

Now you can begin to see how it's possible to
memorize gigantic numbers. You only have to go
through that little journey a couple of times and
translate them back into numbers, and you have
3.14159265358. That didn't take long to do, did it?
Just imagine how far you think you could take that.

If you work it out, all you need is just enough
stages, and once you have those characters sorted
out, you could go on and on. You could easily do
100 digits. Not surprisingly, other people have
already caught on to this, and at the time of this
writing, the world record stands at 70,030 decimal
places to pi. This is held by Suresh Kumar Sharma
from India. I reckon he's using this technique. He
has to be using some sort of journey to do this.

REMEMBERING PHONE NUMBERS

Now you can see how powerful this method is. Of
course you can use it for telephone numbers. Supposing your boss asks you to book a room at the
Waldorf Astoria Hotel. You're on your cell phone,
you have no pen, and he gives you the number.

What's the first thing you do? You think of the hotel. That's the location. That's where you're going to map the images that are about to come up. All right, I'm going to give you the number: 234-3289 (it's not the actual number).

As soon as I read those numbers, I think of these characters. So 23 is Bing Crosby. We could have him at the front entrance of the hotel. He's the doorman. (We're making up a little story here.)

The next set of numbers is 43. To me, that's David Copperfield, so maybe he's in the foyer, performing some sort of magic. Then, maybe at reception, 28, that's comedian Benny Hill. The last digit is 9. If you remember from the number shapes, 9 is a balloon and string. It doesn't take much imagination to picture Benny Hill there, acting the clown and holding a balloon and string.

So for the few seconds it takes to translate those numbers into pictures, you have the telephone number for a long, long time. All you have to do is review it a couple of times, and it's there for life.

Just to recap: Try to turn pairs of numbers into people. Think of associations, maybe Joe Montana from the 49ers for 49, or James Bond for 07. Use the Dominic system to convert numbers into letters; these letters then become initials of famous people or friends. Then you connect these people in a little story or short scene, but anchor it to the associated location.

Let's say you want to remember the number of a computer store. What's the first thing you do? Think of a computer store that you already know; just think of one now. Here's the number: 53-08-15. We won't worry about the seventh digit.

Immediately I think, 53, that's Eric Clapton, so you can have him in the parking lot. Next number, 08; I think of Oliver Hardy. Maybe he's at the front entrance swinging his plank. The, the last digits: 15, Albert Einstein. We could have him at the checkout desk. Of course, he doesn't need any electronic checkout. He has his own chalkboard.

You see what's happening here. You're turning dull, inanimate, unimaginative information, meaningless numbers, into colorful, lively, meaningful, and memorable images.

Here's another for you. Your boss wants you to arrange a lunch with an important client. He says, "Look, can you take this guy to Dino's Italian restaurant?" Think of an Italian restaurant. That's the first thing. You have the location.

He says, "This is the number: 66"—so you think, "Sylvester Stallone. We'll have him as the waiter in the restaurant: 94." That translates to Neil Diamond. We'll have him at the bar serving drinks. Then 72 is the last pair of digits, so we'll

have George Bush in the kitchen cooking up something. So 669472. Just those three people enable
you to remember the number.

For the little time it takes, it could save you
your job. It could even make your career. Sure, you
could always write it down, but isn't it nice to have
that facility, to have that little extra backup should
you need it?

I'm going to give you one more. Let's say you
got an urgent phone call from your wife or your
husband, and they're at the airport. Here's the
number: 36-84-87. What do you do? It's the airport. Well, you think of any location there.

Think of the runway, and 36 is Claudia Schiffer;
84, HD, I think of Humpty Dumpty. So we could
have Claudia Schiffer falling off a wall, Humpty
Dumpty's action, onto the last pair of digits, 87,
Hugh Grant, HG. Claudia Schiffer falling off a wall
on top of Hugh Grant. I don't think Hugh Grant
would complain about that.

It's easy and fun once you've practiced the language of numbers. Not only is it a great mental
exercise, it's extremely practical. It's probably one
of the most valuable tools you can have at your
disposal for number crunching.

Practice with pairs of numbers. Learn your
own language of 100 characters from 00 to 99. See
how your telephone number translates into pic-

tures of people, but above all, have fun. I use it every day.

Test yourself on a regular basis until you automatically see numbers as symbolic characters. Soon you'll find things like telephone numbers, dates, schedules, and so on much easier to remember. Of course, the more you exercise your brain in this way, the more you're going to release of your quantum memory power.

I'll bet you can feel your brain getting stronger already. We'll continue with more exciting quantum memory power techniques in the next chapter.

9
Conquering Your Greatest Fear

What's your greatest fear? In the U.K. at least, next to spiders, the greatest fear is standing up in public and giving a speech. It doesn't matter what the occasion is. Even standing up in front of your own family and friends and just saying a few words can be a devastating experience.

You might be an actor, politician, minister, teacher. At some point in your life, you have to stand up and give a speech. It might be a list of complaints that you want to give to your boss. You work it out carefully. The day comes along. You go in there with good intentions. You're going to get that off your mind, and what happens?

You walk in, and you dry up. Your boss looks at you and says, "What is it?" and all of a sudden you go into a mental blank. The result: opportunity missed.

At some point in our lives, we're given the opportunity to stand up and make our case while others listen. So imagine this. Imagine you're going up to a podium, and there are 200 people in the audience. Your boss and your colleagues are sitting there, and one of your friends says, "Wait a minute; he's forgotten his notes."

They look a bit anxious, but your confidence is supreme. You start delivering your speech in an animated tone, with no hesitations. You start delivering quotes. You ad-lib, and you start telling jokes. Everybody starts laughing with you. Towards the end, you walk down, and everybody cheers. They're impressed. Why? Because you've had no hesitation, no nerves, and more importantly, no notes.

The method I'm going to give you to enable you to do this is as old as the Greeks. If you found some of the other techniques simple to learn, this is equally easy.

Why do we fear giving a speech? Bob Hope once said, "If they like you, they don't applaud. They just let you live." I think it's probably the fear of all eyes on you. You're the center of attention, and you're worried you're going to be the center of ridicule.

Ron, a friend of mine, said that he went on a company course once, and each person in the room had to stand up and talk about themselves, their life history, for about five minutes. Ron's turn was right towards the end, and the nearer it got to his turn, the more he broke into a sweat. Eventually, when he did stand up, he said, "I won't waste your time," and he sat down again.

It can happen to the best of people. Take Steven Spielberg. Once he was giving a speech to students of American law, and he was so gripped with panic that he forgot how to speak English, his own mother tongue. So he started thinking in French just to get some of the words out. This panic attack lasted about a minute or two. Next to insects, public speaking is his greatest fear.

Once Mark Twain had to give a speech about great leaders. He too hated giving speeches, and he said, "Caesar and Hannibal are dead. Wellington has gone to a better place. Napoleon is under the sod, and to be honest, I don't feel too well myself," and he sat down.

The greatest speakers are the ones that have worked at it. I don't believe anybody is a natural speaker. They've had to work at it. Years ago, the thought of having to give a speech would have horrified me, yet now I do it on a regular basis. Can you imagine the World Memory Champion standing up in public with a load of notes? It just wouldn't work. I'd be a laughingstock.

So I have to give speeches. And I can, because I use very simple techniques, the same techniques that I use for memorizing a deck of cards, which I'm going to pass on to you now. It doesn't mean that you have to remember your speech word-for-word, unless of course, you're an actor or you're quoting somebody. An audience wants to hear your interpretation. They want to hear *you*, warts and all. I'm not trying to say that I give the best delivery in the world, but what I can do is use my memory. It enables me to keep eye contact with the audience. That means I'm always involved, and I have control over the audience.

THE MENTAL SPEECH FILE

In a public speaking course, once you've planned your speech, you normally learn to divide it into key points, which you put on cue cards. They could be a list of 10 key points that you can use to keep you on track throughout the speech. This is a lot better than having separate bits of paper that can get all shuffled around, but you can lose the order of cue cards too, or you can lose the cards themselves. The best speakers do it entirely from memory. Enter what I call the *mental speech file*.

Obviously the first thing you have to do is prepare your speech. There are various techniques. One method that I use is called *mind mapping*, which was invented by a guy called Tony Buzan. You get a big sheet of white paper, and you jot down a picture of the theme in the center. If it's a new product, you draw a little picture of it. From there, you chalk out all the ideas. You draw off radiating branches and put in little symbols, little pictures, and try to keep to one word on a branch. Of course, you have subbranches.

At the end of this exercise, you have one sheet of paper with all your thoughts on it. It acts as a sort of mirror for your mind. You can see the whole speech in front of you.

At this point, you can get the structure of the speech; you can see the most important topics. Then you divide them into key points, and guess what you're going to do next. You're going to convert those key points into key images, and of course, the key images then go on a journey.

A JOURNEY WITH DUDLEY MOORE AND GEORGE CLOONEY

By now you're familiar with forming a journey, so I'm going to give you a little exercise. Perhaps you should go back to the journey that you originally devised around your house, because I want you to imagine 10 key images along a journey of 10 stages. If you still have your images from the first exercise in those stages, then put down this book and form another journey, maybe around your place of work.

Once you have your journey sorted out, go to the first stage, and as I feed the information, just use all those skills: Use imagination, association. Use colors, humor, sex, anything that makes you visualize. Associate the key image with the location. OK, here we go.

The first object is a *director's chair*. Fix it, anchor it to the location, and move on to the next stage: *Dudley Moore*. See him there. What's his action? Playing the piano. Move on, and at the next stage, you see a nice, big pile of *money*. Loads of dollars, a big bundle of them.

Move on. This time I want you to picture a big *test tube* bubbling away, the steam coming out of it.

OK, next stage. Now picture a long queue of *smiling, happy faces*. Got that?

Move on to the next stage. This time, picture a *snake charmer* in your mind's eye. Add movement.

Move on, and wherever you are, I want you to bump into a *comedian*. You can make it Jay Leno. What's he doing there? Use logic. Good.

Move on. At this point, I want you to confront the *three wise men* from the Bible.

Move on. Now you meet another character. It's actor *George Clooney*. See if you can picture his face. Again, what's he doing there? What's he wearing?

Finally, the very last stage now, here's the word: *fire*. Whatever you associate with the word *fire*. OK, good.

As always, go back and review the journey. Replay those scenes in your mind. At the first stage, what do you have? A *director's chair*. Next one, somebody playing the piano: *Dudley Moor*e. Next one, a big pile of cash, a bundle of *dollars*. Next one, something bubbling away: a *test tube*. Next stage, a queue of something—yes, *smiling faces*. Next stage, a *snake charmer*. Next, *comedian* Jay Leno. Next, the *three wise men*. Next, *George Clooney*, and finally *fire*. Good.

If you weren't too sure about any of these, then put down the book, go back, and reshoot the scenes. It's a bit like being a film director, and of course, there's no budget on your film. You can spend as much as you like.

When you're sure you have those 10 key images in your head, we can go through a little speech.

REMEMBERING A SPEECH

At this point, I've given you the key images required for the speech that I'm about to give you.

The images should start to make sense once you start reading the speech. See if you can relate the key images to elements of the speech.

You've decided to call a board meeting, and you have your directors there. You want to be promoted to managing director, and this is what you say. Think about the key images that you've memorized.

"Good morning, ladies and gentlemen. The reason I have called this meeting today is that I wish to be promoted from T-boy and general dog's potty to managing director of XYZ Holdings. I have a number of very good reasons why I think I should be promoted. I've been with the company for 10 years and have more experience than the lot of you put together.

"I have produced more profit and developed more products than anyone else. I have a great client base, and I get on well with all our customers. I am charming, witty, wise, and good-looking. Finally, I would just add one very good reason for becoming managing director. My obscenely wealthy uncle has just bought the company outright, and you're all fired."

Let's go through that little tirade and pick out key images. That first line: "Good morning, ladies and gentlemen. The reason I've called this meeting today is I wish to be promoted to managing director." That whole line can be reduced to that one image: *director's chair*.

The next image is *Dudley Moore*. That's to prompt me to say that I've been with the company for 10 years. Remember the Dominic system? Dudley Moore gives you 10, as in the film *10.* "I have a number of very good reasons why I think I should be promoted. I've been with the company for 10 years."

Next one: "I have more experience than the lot of you put together. I have produced more profit," hence the bundle of *dollars*. Now the *test tube* bubbling away—that's research and development: "I've developed more products than anyone else." See how it's fitting together?

Now the queue of *smiling, happy faces*. "I have a great client base, and I get on well with all our customers."

Then comes the series of adjectives: *charming, witty, wise,* and *good-looking*. See how they relate to the key images. First one, *charming*—remember, *snake charmer*. I'm *witty*. That's Jay Leno, the *comedian*. *Wise*: the *three wise men*. *Good-looking*: *George Clooney*. Finally, that last sentence: "I have a very good reason for becoming managing director. My obscenely wealthy uncle has just bought the company outright, and you're all fired." Hence the last key image: *fire*.

The journey ensures that you never forget your way along the speech. It helps you to keep on track with a steady supply of key points. It's a bit like a guide rope.

Other advantages of this technique are that you have eye contact. You have closer contact and involvement with the audience. You feel you have control. You can see them, and of course you sound more convincing. It's more impressive not to use notes, and the audience thinks you're confident about your information, even if you're not. They think you're switched on. The lights are on, and someone's home.

Just think of the times you can use this method. You can use it to remember jokes. Maybe you have to give a speech at the House of Representatives. What about being father of the bride or best man at a wedding? They can be harrowing times. Maybe you have an important product announcement or a grievance with your boss. You can walk in cool, calm, and collected: "I'd like to clear the air on a number of points." The last thing your boss wants to see is a load of cue cards or bits of paper. If you can walk in and deliver your tirade, that'll impress your boss.

A speech mental file is a bit like an autocue. It's like your own foolproof idiot board. I don't know if you've noticed, but politicians these days have their own transparent idiot boards. It allows them to read the information from a script, but they can also keep eye contact with the audience.

The key images along the journey give you total control. You're always one step ahead, because you can see the key images coming off in front of you. If you do forget one of those images, it probably indicates that the information wasn't that important in the first place. Of course, you can always keep a separate sheet. Not that you'll ever need it, but it's comforting to know that in the worst case, should you dry up, you can always refer to your notes.

Once you've prepared your speech and you've converted it into key images, all you need to do is run through that journey a couple of times back to front, and you have it in your head.

Sometimes you can get distracted, but you always know from your internal mental geography where you are. This technique allows you to deviate. Sometimes if I'm giving a speech, somebody will ask a question. It might be an interesting one, and we can deviate and go off on a tangent, but I know when to come back.

It's a bit like going on the motorway. You see an interesting attraction, so you decide to get off, but you make a note of the exit. It's exit 10, so you know where to go back on. It's the same thing with this journey.

Remember also that a successful speech has a starting place, points along the way, and a concluding destination. If you think about it, a speech is a journey in itself, so use the journey method.

REMEMBERING QUOTES

What about quotes? If you want to throw in the odd quote, then simply break down that specific quote into a memorable miniscene or ministory, and have it take place at the relevant stage of the journey.

Let's say you're giving a speech to children about the merits of learning, and you want to throw in the following quote from Aristotle: "The roots of education are bitter, but the fruit is sweet."

You can get a nice key image from that. You might imagine an apple tree with a schoolboy climbing up it to get an apple. You simply slot that into the relevant point along your journey. If you really get keen on quotes, you might want to mentally store them all in one building or in an area like a museum or a library.

Here are some examples. How would you visualize this? Here's one from Oscar Wilde: "Art never expresses anything but itself." Any thoughts? I see a picture within a picture.

A LIBRARY EXERCISE

We're going to do yet another exercise. This time I'm going to give you five quotes to remember, and I want you to store them in one area. Why don't you pick your local library? Just form a little journey of five stages around your library. You're going through the entrance, and then passing the desk, and so on. When you're ready, you can read on.

I'm going to give you some images now. Go to the first stage. Picture this. A *movie*, whatever comes to mind. Go to the second stage: *computer*. Third stage: *telephone*. Fourth stage: *aircraft*. Finally, *oil well*. Got those? Quickly go through them again: *movie*, *computer*, *telephone*, *aircraft*, and *oil well*.

You're thinking, "What's he up to now? What is he having me memorize now?"

Do you ever listen to somebody telling jokes, and you think, "I wish I could remember those. I know the actual content of the jokes, but I wish I could just get a trigger for each one of them." This journey method gives you a trigger for remembering the quotes or jokes. These are some of my favorite "bad quotes."

The first one: *movie*. Here's one from H. M. Warner of Warner Brothers in 1927. This was just about when sound was being introduced to moving pictures. He said, "Who the hell wants to hear actors talk?"

Next your image was *computer*. This is a great one. "I think there is a world market for maybe five computers." This was Thomas Watson, the chairman of IBM, in 1943. What a great prediction that was.

Next one. This is *telephone*. "This telephone has too many shortcomings to be seriously considered as a means of communication. The device is inherently of no value to us." This was in a Western Union internal memo from 1876.

What's your next key image? *Aircraft*. All right. This was Lord Kelvin, the president of the Royal Society in 1895, and this was his prediction: "Heavier-than-air flying machines are impossible."

The last one is *oil well*. This was from drillers whom Edwin L. Drake tried to enlist for his project to drill for oil in 1859. This is what they said: "Drill for oil? You mean drill into the ground to try and find oil? You're crazy."

You might need to read over the quote a few times, but that single key image will act as a trigger for you to recall the whole thing, and you can use it for jokes as well.

ACING A TOUGH JOB INTERVIEW

Here's some quantum memory power techniques to help you get through a job interview. Before I took up work as a memory man, I applied for a job at Stansted Airport in London.

During the interview, the guy said, "Look, Mr. O'Brien, if you're successful at getting this job, you'll need to know the phonetic alphabet. Are you familiar with that?"

"Well," I said, "I've heard of it, but I don't really know it."

He gave me a piece of paper and said, "Look, you have to read down there. A is alpha, B is bravo, C is Charlie," and so on. He said, "If you want the job, you're going to have to learn this for a second interview. I'm going to give you the piece of paper now. You're going to take it away, come back, and we'll test you on it. You have to know it for the job."

As he was talking to me, I'd already starting memorizing the information. By the time he got to the end of it and handed me the paper, I said, "Right, I think I have that," and gave it back to him.

"No, no," he said. "You don't understand. I want you to take this away and just learn it at your leisure."

"I've just learned it."

"What? If I say Q, what's that?"

"That's Quebec."

"So what's R?"

"Romeo."

"OK. Can you go through the list?"

"Yes. Alpha, bravo, Charlie, delta, echo, foxtrot, golf, hotel—"

"That's great. How the hell did you do that?"

"I just have a pretty good memory. I'll go backwards if you like. Zulu, Yankee, X-ray—"

"No, no," he said. "That won't be necessary. You got the job."

Being able to do that was the icing on the cake, and you can do that with a trained memory and a mental fact file. Before the interview, as I was swotting, I was converting facts and figures and putting them into key images along a mental journey.

Put yourself in the shoes of the interviewer. Wouldn't you be impressed that someone had bothered to do a little research about the background of your company? He comes across as intelligent and enthusiastic, and he's asking all the right questions.

What about your CV, your curriculum vitae or résumé? It's worth taking the time to memorize your own history. You can put it in order by using key images again and using a journey. This prevents ums and uhs and "I can't really remember what I was doing then." Interviewers don't like gaps in people's history.

The mental fact file helps to order your thoughts efficiently. The worst thing that can happen is having your mind go blank just when you need to give a good impression. You may find that you need one or two journeys: one for your CV, another one for the details of the company. There really is no limit to the amount of information you can store. You have financial figures, balance sheet, customers, key employees, even share prices.

A word of warning here: don't reel off figures for the entire interview. The guy might think you're a nut, or you may unnerve him into thinking that you're after his job.

Another piece of advice, which my father gave me once: when promulgating your esoteric cogitations, beware of platitudinous ponderosities. Let your conversation possess clarified conciseness with concatenated cogency. Eschew all battlement, but above all, don't use big words.

Keep the language simple. What are you trying to do? Are you trying to land the job or confuse the interviewer with words you don't understand yourself?

In any event, you could use a journey around the job location. Use all the tools available to you—mnemonics, number shapes, number rhymes for numbers, or even the Dominic system. You could use the methods on the names and faces. That alone could land you the job.

It really is a competitive market out there, so why don't you give yourself an unfair advantage over the rest of the pack and land the one job that everyone else is after? It's easy. See if you can memorize your own curriculum vitae or résumé by turning aspects of your life into colorful, meaning-ful images.

Just to recap: to memorize your speech, first condense the contents into key points. Then cre-ate symbols for each key point by using imagina-tive, colorful, meaningful, key images. Place each key image at various stages along a familiar mental journey. The journey will act as a guide, ensuring that you don't confuse the order of your speech or lose your place. It's your very own mental speech file, an invisible autocue.

Don't try to memorize your speech word for word. The audience wants to hear you, with your spontaneity, mistakes and all. Use a mental fact file for storing data in preparation for a job interview, facts and figures about the company, your own cur-riculum vitae or résumé, and so on. These can all be stored using key images and a mental journey.

10

A Journey of 31 Stages

Have you noticed that these days we seem to be under more and more time pressure? We seem to rely more on our smartphones, electronic organizers—you name it. I think this has contributed to a steady decline in our ability to memorize things. We just don't need to exercise our minds so much.

The Japanese, in contrast, although they're keen on electronics, are very well organized. They seem to rely more on their memories than we do. They seem to do away with appointment books. Appointment books are great, but what happens if you lose them, or maybe the battery goes on the blink on your smartphone?

Anyway, wouldn't it be nice to have full control over your appointments, to know exactly in an instant what you're supposed to be doing on a certain day? Well, you can, with a mental diary.

By using a journey of 31 stages, you can tell at a glance what treats lie in store. Each stage of the journey represents a day of the month, and appointments are placed at the corresponding stages. For example, let's say you have an appointment with your dentist on January 5. At the fifth stage of the journey, you see your dentist standing in anticipation with a drill.

I have a journey. It's 31 stages, and it starts at the top of a hill, and it looks over an old village I used to live in. In fact, I was born there. It's the village of Bramley, in southern England. This is how it goes.

I'm at the top of the hill, and there's an old ruin—an old tower. Then it goes on, there's a little tree stump, which I use as a stage. Then it goes on to a well, a secret tunnel, a garden fence that leads into a garden.

Then there's the driveway of an old mansion. There's a stile, and then there's another tree, where I used to take picnics as a child. There's an old shed, and so the journey goes.

Eventually you get to the 27th stage, and there's a gas station. A restaurant is the 30th stage, and finally, the last stage, the 31st, is a church.

How can we use this to keep an appointment book? Suppose you have to return a library book on the 27th. In my case, the 27th stage is a gas station, so I'd visualize a big book leaning up against the gas pumps at the gas station.

Another example: let's say I have a ticket to see an ABBA tribute band. (Yes, I'm a bit of an ABBA freak, I'm afraid.) To remember that, I imagine the group, the original group, walking into the restaurant, because the 30th stage of my route is a restaurant. Also, if you want to add details of times or quantity, what do you do? You use number shapes, or the Dominic system.

For example, if I want to remember the ABBA concert starts at 8:00 p.m., I use the number shape for 8, which is, if you remember, a snowman. I'd introduce the snowman into the picture; I'd have it standing outside the restaurant. Now I can't forget. ABBA, that has to be the 30th, because it's the restaurant. What time is it? Think of the snowman: it has to be 8:00 p.m.

Again, I know that the dentist appointment is January 5, because my dentist is standing there at the 5th stage. Well, what if the appointment is at 3:00? I'd have him standing with a pair of handcuffs. Remember, the number shape for 3 is handcuffs. Perhaps he's intending to keep me there in that chair whether I like it or not.

So I can survey the whole month ahead by looking down on the village of Bramley; I can see all 31 stages at once. You should try this yourself. Maybe look at a favorite walk that you literally know backwards and forwards, so after a while you get to know that at the 15th stage is the garage, and the 2nd stage is the parking lot.

As you already know, the journey preserves the order of events, and therefore the appointments that lie on them. Of course, you want to keep an ordinary appointment book, but isn't it nice to have that element of control? You could also be out and about and bump into somebody. They might say, "Are you doing something on the 14th?" Instead of saying, "I have to check my calendar," you consult your own powerful internal calendar— your memory.

CONQUERING THE LIST DISEASE

Now you know how to remember appointments. What about everyday chores and tasks that we never get around to doing? "I must cut the grass. I must do something about the woodworm in the kitchen table. I must drop in on the old lady at the end of the road. I must join the health club." Don't those tasks seem to add up, and you never get around to doing any of them?

This can all become a bit stressful. You start to exaggerate the problem—"there are so many things I should be doing"—even though you can probably count them on the fingers of one hand.

The answer, of course, is to organize your chores by writing them down, which is why we've become a nation of list makers. Even this practice is not without its stresses. Bits of paper can get lost. Worse still, you can become an obsessive list maker, buying truckloads of Post-it pads and plastering your walls with memoranda. In extreme cases, you draw up the mother of all lists once a morning, detailing the lists that you must write during the day.

Let me suggest a calming and effective alternative: the mental in-tray. Again, choose a simple journey with 10 stages. It's important that the place holds happy memories for you. Why not use somewhere from your honeymoon (providing it wasn't a disaster) or a scene from your childhood? I use a hotel that I stayed at on a great holiday. This time, instead of getting you to form a journey, I want you to go on a journey with me at that holiday resort.

Try to picture this with me. I'm going to give you 10 stages now. First stage: a *sunny beach*. Now just walk back there for a bit, and there's a *bar* just edging onto that beach. Behind the bar is a *restaurant*, which is the third stage. If you step out through the window, that will take you onto the *hotel drive.*

Going up from the drive, you come to the *main reception.* We're on stage 5 at the moment. Going on from there, you're now in the *lounge,* and from the lounge, you see a *pool.* At the back of the pool, there's a window leading into the *bedroom,* and just back from the bedroom, there's a *Jacuzzi,* which leads onto the *balcony.*

We're going to need to go through this again. With me, just imagine this. A sunny *beach,* in back of it a *bar,* then a *restaurant.* You go through the window to the *hotel drive.* It takes you to the *reception area.* Then through to the *lounge.* The lounge backs onto the *pool;* the pool backs onto the *bedroom.* Just to the back of that there's a *Jacuzzi,* and then a *balcony.* Got that?

With that very pleasant setting in mind, we can now place 10 key images for typical chores you might have. Go back to the sunny beach. This time I want you to picture your *bank manager* lazing in the sun. Picture your bank manager on the sunny beach. That's to remind you that you have to make a withdrawal.

Now go back to the *bar.* This time I want you to imagine that your *plumber* is there. That's to remind you that there's a leak in the bathroom, and you have to fix that.

Next stage is the *restaurant*. Just picture your *lawnmower* on one of the tables there. What's that to remind you? You have to cut the grass.

Go through the window of the restaurant to the *hotel drive*. There you see a large, dirty *ashtray*. That's to remind you that you have to stop smoking.

What's the next stage? It's the *reception area*. Picture your *aunt* in tears. That's to remind you that it's about time you sent a letter to her.

Now you go to the *lounge*. This time, picture *Superman in a phone booth*. That should tell you that it's time to pay your phone bill.

Now we go to the *pool* area. In the pool is a *car*. That's a trigger to remind you that you have to renew your car registration.

The pool backs onto the bedroom. In the bedroom is a *shopping cart*. Picture that. It's wrapped up in the bedclothes, and that's to remind you to do some shopping. Two more stages to go.

In the *Jacuzzi* is a *camera*. You have to develop those photos. Finally, on the *balcony*, there's your *vacuum cleaner*. Yes, you have to vacuum the house.

See how many of those you can remember. It doesn't matter if you can't; it's just to demonstrate the principle of this mental in-tray.

Back to the sunny *beach*. Who's there? *Bank manager*: make the withdrawal. At the *bar*, your *plumber*. Yes, you have to get that bathroom leak fixed. At the *restaurant*, what do you see? The *lawnmower*. You have to cut the grass. *Hotel drive*, that's right: you have to stop smoking. It's the dirty *ashtray*.

Who is that in tears at *reception*? Letter to relative. In the *lounge*, you have to pay the phone bill, and that's *Superman in the phone box*. In the *pool* is your *car*. You have to renew your registration. In the *bedroom*, wrapped up in the bedclothes, yes, it's the *shopping cart*. You have to do your shopping. *Jacuzzi*: develop those *photos*; it's the *camera*. Finally, what do you have to do in the *house*? You have to *vacuum* it.

Can you see how the journey is preserved in the order of the things you have to do? Your mental in-tray. The image of a supermarket cart tucked up in bed, bizarre as it is, can mean only one thing: it's your turn to do the shopping. The sight of your aunt in tears can only mean one thing: it's about time you sent her a letter.

Priority is not that important. Once you have all your worries out in the open and blended with the pleasant surroundings of your journey, you'll have an equal awareness of each of them, which will allow you to put them into better perspective.

A mental in-tray has many uses. I use it when I'm attending a meeting or have an important phone conversation. If there are certain key points that I want to convey, I translate those into images and place them along my in-tray journey. There's nothing more frustrating than the sudden realization (usually on your way home) that you've forgotten to make your most important point at a crucial meeting.

I use the mental in-tray last thing at night as well. If I must leave a note for the milkman, I imagine a bottle of milk at stage 1. The accountant, pictured at stage 2, reminds me I have to call him, and the gas meter at stage 3 reminds me that I have to pay my heating bill.

Here's one thing that you might miss by using this technique: when you have a list of things to do, isn't it nice to strike the items off? Yes, I have the plumber sorted out. Yes, I've cut the grass. Yes, I have the car registered. Tick that one off.

Every time you do a chore with your mental in-tray, just throw an imaginary hand grenade at it. Like your bank manager on the beach—just blow him up into oblivion. You've done that; you've withdrawn the money. Throw a hand grenade at the vacuum cleaner, because you've vacuumed the house. It's a great feeling.

AN ASSOCIATION EXERCISE

Now we have another exercise. This is going to be a limbering exercise for your powers of association. I'm going to give you some pairs of words or objects, with some people thrown in. The idea is, as quickly as you like, to make a connection between each of the words or each of the objects. Here we go:

Apple, rainbow
Canoe, Bette Davis
Dracula, fire extinguisher
Zebra, yellow
Train, Cleopatra
Telephone, hot air balloon
Desk, waterfall
Hat, bow and arrow
Computer, umbrella
Scarf, streaker
A pair of ice skates, Rambo
Sandwich, lamppost
Beach ball, Napoleon
Pencil, rocket
Microphone, penguin
Book, trapeze
George Bush, see-through negligee
boxer shorts, Velcro
Hammer, gorilla
Cannonball, Madonna

At this point I suspect you have some rather interesting images in your head. If you really made the connection—and it should have been fairly immediate—let's see if you can connect one word to the other. Below I'm going to give a clue, and see if you can come up with the paired word. Jot it down next to the clue, or write this list down on a piece of paper and do the same.

Yellow	Sandwich
Apple	Umbrella
Dracula	Napoleon
Canoe	Pencil
Hot air balloon	Penguin
Cleopatra	Book
Desk	See-through negligee
Bow and arrow	Velcro
Streaker	Gorilla
Rambo	Cannonball

Just make a note of the ones that you can't remember. Maybe you weren't using enough imagination. If not, change the connection by changing the image.

Can you see that by creating these images, it's fairly easy to come up with associations? I'm not expecting you to get 100 percent correct, but it's a great exercise for oiling the wheels of association.

NUMBER EXERCISES

Now we're going to do some number exercises. Again, I want you to form a journey of 10 stages. I'm going to give you some numbers, and I want you to convert them into number shapes, so when you read the number 3, you think of *handcuffs*, and number 2, *swan*.

First stage: 8. Second stage: 0. Keep moving on. Third stage: 0 again. Fourth stage: 5. Moving on: 2, 5, 9, 0, 0 again, and finally, 0 again.

OK, rewind the mental video tape. Go through the scenes, go through the stages, and what do you have? Was it a snowman for the first one, 8? Next stage, football, 0; 0 again. Then did you have a curtain hook for 5, a swan for 2, the 5 again? A balloon and string for 9. Then you had a 0, 0, and finally 0.

This is all about how to learn any subject. Can you remember out of all those hours you spent as a student—probably about 10,000—how many were actually spent in learning how to learn? Can you recall a single lesson devoted to memory techniques? How many hours did you spend on the art of concentration? Did you ever have a lesson on the art of observation? What about visualization or mnemonics to help you memorize things? If the answer is no, you can't remember, neither can I.

When I was at school struggling away, I was expected to get on as best I could. Nobody ever taught me how to learn in the first place. I wasn't a natural, as you probably guessed from my school reports. Sadly, I didn't enjoy school. The whole learning process for me was an uphill struggle. I now believe that every child should have to be taught how to learn.

I have a phrase which says, "Teach the teachers how to teach the children how to learn." There should be training for all students, at least once a month, preferably first thing on a Monday morning, on how to learn.

I get letters and emails from people all over. Many of them say, "I got your book," or, "I got your course. I passed my exams with flying colors." But they also say, "Dominic, why don't they teach this stuff at school?" It's a good question, and it beats the hell out of me.

I dropped out of school when I was 16 because I couldn't hack studying any longer. I just didn't know how to absorb the knowledge in the first place. Now I get parents sending their children to me—to me, that dyslexic kid from 1967. I'm teaching them how to learn. There's a certain irony in all this. I never realized that learning could be such fun.

Earlier, we touched on mnemonics. As you remember, mnemonic is any device that aids memory. "Richard of York goes battling in vain" gives you the colors of the rainbow.

Here's another one. "Every good boy deserves favor." If you take the first letter of each of those words, you get E-G-B-D-F. These are the line notes in the treble clef.

You can make up a lot of ditties to remember anything. Take physics, for example. This is my favorite: volts equals amps times resistance: $V = A \times R$. All you have to think of is, "Virgins are rare," and you're not likely to forget that.

Here's another one, which uses rhyme. "Columbus sailed the ocean blue in 1492." Mnemonics are a favorite for medical students as well. They're great fun if you want to convert chemical symbols, atomic weights, or historical dates into images.

Let's take geography, for example. I used to hate that subject. I got the lowest grade, but I wish I were back at school now.

Let's talk about countries and capitals. The idea is to make a link between the country and its capital. For instance, the capital of the Philippines is Manila. How would you make a connection there? I think of a friend of mine called Philip pining because he's a man that's ill. *Philip pines, man ill.* It's a little far-fetched, but there is definitely a chain of links.

Let's have a look at the capital of Switzerland, which is Bern. Imagine the Swiss have come up with a new ritual. They stand at the top of the mountain and expose a *bare knee* as they're yodeling. It's a quick, immediate association. The capital of Switzerland is Bern. It's a little bit like an old Monty Python sketch showing a guy at the top of a snow-capped mountain, baring one knee and yodeling.

That's another thing that you should use: humor. We tend to want to return to happy memories. If you make connections attractive in the process—in other words, you're producing happy juice in your brain—you have more chance of returning to them later.

The capital of Afghanistan is Kabul. Imagine that all the cars are driven by bulls. Get inventive. There's always a link if you allow your mind to find one.

Let's take New Zealand. The capital of New Zealand is Wellington. If, by a little stretch of the imagination, you were to turn New Zealand upside down, it could look like the shape of a wellington boot. Sometimes that's all you need to go on.

The capital of Australia is Canberra, not Sydney. Again, by a little stretch of the imagination, if you look at the map of Australia, it vaguely looks like the shape of a camera.

Here's another one. The capital of Grenada is St. George's. What do you think of? When I hear the name *St. George's*, I think of St. George slaying a dragon, but this time he has modern weaponry: he's using a grenade. Grenada, St. George's.

Let's have a look at the American states. Again, just allow yourself to find a link. Try to make the connections fairly immediate. Use all the tools available to you. Use your senses, imagination, exaggeration, humor, sex if you like, color, movement, sight, sound, smell, taste, and touch.

It doesn't matter if you already know what the capital is. I'm going to give you one now. The capital of Mississippi is Jackson. To me, it's a straightforward connection. I imagine seeing Michael Jackson wading through the Mississippi trying to get to the other side.

The capital of New York is Albany. Again, I try to pick out a feature. So I imagine the Statue of Liberty with long, flowing *auburn* hair. It's not exactly *Albany*, but it's just enough to trigger the name. Statue of Liberty, auburn; New York, Albany.

Another one: Kentucky; the capital is Frankfort. I think of Kentucky Fried Chicken, but they've run out of chicken, so they've opted for frankfurters.

The capital of Utah is Salt Lake City. A connection that comes to mind straightaway: imagine being told that you had to tar the entire area of Salt Lake City. *You tar*: Utah, Salt Lake City.

With some of these states and capitals, you have to get a little bit more inventive. Take South Dakota. The capital of South Dakota is Pierre. When I hear South Dakota, I think of those presidential carvings on Mount Rushmore. So picture a *pier* jutting out from the carvings, and put yourself there. See yourself coming out on this pier. Immerse yourself in the scene. South Dakota, Pierre.

If you create images like that, you're never going to forget them, and of course, you're engaging the whole of your brain. Your right brain is involved. It's become active in the learning process. We'll be looking at the individual functions of the left and the right hemisphere later on.

Let's take another one: Montana. Helena is the capital. I don't really know Montana. I can't think of a place connected with it, but I know the name *Helena*. She used to be an old girlfriend of mine, so I imagine her playing the card game *Montana Red Dog*. Now I have a connection. I've bridged the gap.

I once had to do a TV show in Scotland, and they issued a challenge to me. They gave me somebody from the audience. They said, "Can you teach this guy how to memorize the American states?"

"Well," I said, "we'll give it go." I fed him all 50 American states and their capitals. We were given about 25 minutes to do it. I went back on set—it was live—and they started rolling the cameras. This guy went through every single state. I couldn't believe it. He wasn't supposed to do that in 25 minutes.

I wonder how fast you can wade through the American states. Do you remember the old-fashioned way, where you had to keep repeating information? With this method, you can go right through all 50. OK, you might get a few wrong, but judge for yourself. How much faster is this method?

Let's test you. What's the capital of Mississippi? Got the image? Michael Jackson. What's the capital of New York? Think of the Statue of Liberty. Albany. The capital of Kentucky? Frankfort.

Now what happened to South Dakota with the monument? It's a pier; that's it. Montana, Helena. Still have those countries? What's the capital of Switzerland? Bern. Afghanistan? Kabul.

All the time you're doing this, you're oiling the memory machine. You're exercising creativity. You're allowing your imagination to do what it's best at doing: being highly inventive. You're freeing up the mechanism by which memory works—association—and it's starting to get faster.

Not only are you exercising your memory so that it becomes more efficient in many ways, you're also becoming smarter, because you're gaining knowledge. Associations are starting to become automatic. Sometimes it's so fast that you don't even know how you've come up with one.

For example, this happened to me with Maine and Augusta. I suddenly thought of a lion. Maine made me think of a lion's mane. August: I thought of Leo, because in August the sun in in the zodiac sign of Leo. Now I have the connection. Bingo: Leo the Lion.

AN EXERCISE WITH THE AMERICAN STATES

Now that we have the wheels of association working in your mind, let's give you another exercise. I'm going to feed you 10 American states and their capitals. As fast as you like, come up with an association. It doesn't matter how you get there as long as you make a link. Let's make a start:

Alabama, Montgomery
Alaska, Juneau
Delaware, Dover
Idaho, Boise
Kansas, Topeka
Louisiana, Baton Rouge
Michigan, Lansing
South Carolina, Columbia
Texas, Austin
West Virginia, Charleston

OK, let's see how you did. I'm going to give you the capitals this time, and you give me the state. You can jot down the answers below, or write the capitals down on a piece of paper and add in the states.

Montgomery
Juneau
Dover
Boise
Topeka
Baton Rouge
Lansing
Columbia
Austin
Charleston

Did that work for you? You can find more examples. If you're feeling really keen, look up the state capitals on the Internet, write them down, and go through all 50 states.

MEMORIZING THE PERIODIC TABLE OF ELEMENTS

I once had to do a phone-in on television for students for studying exams. I was giving them tips. It was live on a television program in Liverpool, and the TV company faxed me the periodic table of all the elements from hydrogen right up to ununoctium, element number 110. They sent me the facts rather late. I got in a taxi and got on the plane at Heathrow; by the time I arrived in Liverpool, I'd gotten that information in my head. They also wanted me to memorize the atomic weights, like hydrogen, whose weight is 1.00797.

I prepared a journey with 110 stages, and I just imagined seeing each element as a key image. If, for instance, I was asked what the element number 36 was, I'd say it was krypton, and the weight was 83.80, or bismuth is element number 83; I could say that's Bi, the symbol, and it's 208.98.

This may sound impressive, but I have a trained memory. I'm equipped to do this, and you can be too. Again, speed comes with practice. Always use the three ingredients: association, location, imagination.

Let's simplify chemistry a bit. Let's take the symbol for tin, which is Sn. How would you find a connection between *tin* and *Sn*? I think of the French cartoon character Tintin, who had a dog named Snowy. If you allow it to, your mind can find a connection.

The symbol for lead is Pb. I think of a lead-weighted plumb line. Actually, the Latin for *lead* is *plumbum.* For gold, the symbol is Au. I think that gold has a certain aura about it.

How about mercury? That symbol is Hg. Again, if you look for a connection, you'll find it. When I see *Hg*, I think of author H. G. Wells. How would you connect that with mercury? Just imagine a *well* being contaminated with *mercury*. Hg, mercury.

TACKLING DEFINITIONS

How can you tackle definitions? Let's take alcohol—my favorite. Alcohol is a series of compounds of carbon, hydrogen, and oxygen. If you think of those letters, C, H, and O, and then think of alcohol as *causing hangovers*, CHO, you'll always remember this definition.

Here's another. An allotrope is an element that can exist in different forms, like carbon. Carbon can be tough, like diamond, or it can be soft, like graphite, so it has many allotropic forms. Think of different forms of shapes out of a rope, a lot of a rope tricks—allotropic.

Get your children on to this now. They'll mop up the periodic table, and just imagine how useful that would be for learning chemistry. Every time you hear the name of an element, you're already familiar with it, and you know its atomic number. Once you train your memory, you could learn it in a day.

Just to demonstrate the principle of learning these elements, I want you to form another journey, let's say around your old chemistry lab, if you can remember that, or maybe the grounds of your school. I'm going to feed you first 10 elements in order, but first we're going to need some associations.

When I say the word *hydrogen*, just think of an explosion, a hydrogen bomb. For *helium*, think of a helium balloon, lighter than air. *Lithium*, what's the nearest thing you have to that? How about a *lighter*? For *beryllium*, which is the 4th element, think of somebody you know called *Beryl*.

Boron: think of boring a *hole*. For *carbon*, which is the 6th item, think of a *pencil*. *Nitrogen*: I think of someday rowing in the night (*night row*), so think of a *canoe*. *Oxygen*: think of an *oxygen mask*. *Fluorine*, imagine some *flour*, and finally, for *neon*, the 10th element, think of a bright *neon light*.

Now you have ready-made associations, so you need to put them in a location. Set down this book and work out a mental journey around your school. When you're ready, start reading again.

Are you ready with those 10 stages now? Immerse yourself in the first stage, and when you read the element, visualize its association. Here we go:

Hydrogen	Carbon
Helium	Nitrogen
Lithium	Oxygen
Beryllium	Fluorine
Boron	Neon

Now go back to the first stage. Just let the images wash over you. You're at the first stage of the journey. What do you see? You should be seeing an explosion: hydrogen. Next stage, something floating: a balloon, helium. Next stage, lithium. Keep going now: beryllium, boron, carbon, nitrogen, oxygen, fluorine, and that neon light—neon.

Again, if you'd made a little marker along your journey so that you know where the 5th stage is, which is where the boron is, I could say to you, "Give me the 4th element, atomic number 4." From your internal geography, you'd say, "Beryllium." You just have to go back one stage from boron.

If I say, "Give me the 7th element," you go 2 forward from boron, which gives you nitrogen. If you really wanted to be smart, you'd go backwards. You'd go neon, fluorine, oxygen, and so on.

Really, this is the key to learning to learn. Always look for associations, and make connections the whole time in whatever you're learning. After a while, it's going to become automatic. Practice.

You can go through all 50 states. When it comes to chemistry, don't look at them as boring old elements. Bring them to life. Animate them. Think of hydrogen as a hydrogen bomb, but above all, enjoy learning.

11

Some Words on Words

. . . .

Now we're going to talk about words and their meanings, and then we're going to take an interplanetary journey. I'm going to say a word or two on a word or two. This is going to be really rich, coming from a self-confessed dyslexic, but I'm going to tell you how to learn how to spell correctly.

Actually, I believe I'm an ex-dyslexic, but I still have to be careful about certain words and their meanings. like the difference between *annual* and *perennial* or *lightning* and *lightening*. It's probably because I found spelling and certain meanings difficult when I was in school. I've had to work hard to overcome this difficulty.

So there you are, lying in bed, doing a crossword, and all of a sudden you come across a word you're not sure of. You look up the meaning, but you've forgotten it the following morning.

Do you remember when we were memorizing names and faces? The trick was to forge a link, albeit an artificial one, between the person's face and name.

The same principle applies with words and their meanings. Take the word *garrulous*, which means *talkative*. As far as I can see, there is no obvious link between these words; they certainly don't sound similar. The only thing they have in common is that each has three syllables, so you need to call upon your inexhaustible supply of creative imagination.

Let's think of a link. How about *Gary talks a lot*? Not only does it sound like *garrulous*, but we've rather sneakily put in the meaning of the word as well. *Garrulous, Gary talks a lot, talkative*. In effect, *Gary talks a lot* is acting as a bridge between the word we want to understand and its meaning.

How would you construct a mental bridge between *cacophony* and its meaning, which is a *harsh sound*? Cacophony: harsh sound. Think of the cackling of hens. That makes a pretty harsh sound. *Cacophony, cackle of hens, cacophony*.

Here's another sound meaning. *Vociferous* means *loud* or *noisy*. So just think of a *voice ferocious*: vociferous.

Here's another. *Largesse* means *bestowal of gifts.* I think of the words *large* and the *dollar sign.* So you have large dollar sign: $, *ess.* Imagine bestowing someone with a gift of a large number of dollars.

Here's another: *impasse.* Impasse is a position from which progress is impossible. We've all had situations like that. Think of *impossible to pass*: *impasse.*

Here are a few more examples for you. *Exigent* means *urgent, demanding action.* I think of an announcement: *exit, gents, urgent.*

Eclectic: selecting from a variety of sources. *He collects it all: eclectic.*

How about *parity*? That means *equality in status.* Think of level—*par, parity.*

How about *factitious*? That means *contrived, produced artificially.* So think of *fact, fictitious.*

SPELLING

What about spelling? I say *potato*, you say *potahto*, but how do you spell it? Is it with or without an E?

With any word you're not sure of, you have to get inventive. Create a reminder. Think of "Not one single potato has an E in it, but two do." In other words, the only time you stick an E in is with plurals.

Here are some common words people have trouble spelling.

Separate. When you think of it, you may ask, is it spelled *separate* or *separate*?

Here's another for you: *anoint.* Does that have 2 Ns or 3? It has one N to begin with, so it's *anoint.*

Another one: *receive.* I before E except after C.

Another one: *cemetery.* There's no A in the word *cemetery*, if that was what you were wondering.

Embarrassed has 2 Rs and 2 Ss.

Here's another one: *pursue.*

Accommodate: that has 2 Cs and 2 Ms.

Accidentally. It's not *accidently*, though people sometimes pronounce it that way. It's *accident-ally* with *-ally* at the end.

Desperate—not *desparate.*

Finally, *definitely.* If you think there's an A in it, you're wrong.

As before, you need to be a little bit inventive. So let's take those words.

Separate. It's *para* in the middle, so imagine somebody in a parachute descending upon the word *separate.* The parachutist is separating the word: *para.*

What about *anoint*? Just think of *an ointment*, and then you can't get the spelling wrong.

Receive: I before E except after C.

What about *cemetery*? There's no A in it. It's all Es. If you look at the word *cemetery*, there's a sort of symmetry about it. The symmetry of *cemetery*.

How can you remember that there are 2 Rs and 2 Ss in *embarrassed*? You're embarrassed, so you're *rose red* and *feeling an ass*. Rose red—two Rs—and *ass* has 2 Ss in it. So 2 Rs, 2 Ss.

Here's another one. *Pursue*: how can you remember that it's not *persue*? Imagine being *pursued* by a thief who's after your *purse*.

Accommodate. Think of *accommodation*. Think of taking your company car, CC, to the Motorway Motel, MM.

Accidentally: think of having an accident in an alley. Accident, alley.

How will you get *desperate*? Think of *desperado*.

Finally, what about *definitely*? Think of this. Night follows day as day follows night; in other words, as D-E follows N-I-T-E.

As you're doing this, not only are you picking up valuable learning skills, but you're also exercising and developing the whole of your brain. You may notice already that you're slightly quicker at brainstorming, and ideas are coming to the fore faster. Your memory craves imagination and making associations.

So help your vocabulary by linking a word with its meaning, and look for patterns or clues to help act as reminders for spelling. Are there 2 Ts in *battalion* or one? Think of doing *battle*, B-A-T-T, and *battalion*, preparing to do battle, and that should give you the answer.

LEARNING A FOREIGN LANGUAGE

You could use this same technique for learning a foreign language. Think how much easier, faster, and more fun it would be to munch your way through 50, 100, 1,000 words of Spanish, French, or German. I teach this method to students, and they tell me, "How did I ever manage before?"—endlessly slugging away as they did with repetition after repetition, and still a lot of the words didn't sink in.

Yes, sure, using this method, you'll still have to review or revise. Remember the Ebbinghaus rule of 5? Review something 5 times and you have it for life, but this method takes away the monotony of endless repetition, because although the words and meaning will become automatic after a while, the use of images is so powerful that you'll triple or quadruple the rate at which you absorb foreign words and their meanings.

For example, the Spanish for *cow* is *vaca*. Imagine a crazy scene of a cow vacuuming a field.

How would you remember that the German for *rain* is *regen*? Simple. Find a link between the foreign word and its meaning, no matter how bizarre. I picture a shower of Ronald Reagans falling from the sky. It's the sort of thing you might expect from a surrealist painting, a René Magritte or a Salvador Dali.

The French for *pink* is *rose*. Picture a bright, pink rose. The clue is always in the word. You only have to allow your imagination to find one.

A FRENCH TEST

Let's do a fun exercise to help you with vocabulary in French. I'm going to give you an English word, and then I'm going to give you the French equivalent, and you're going to try and find a link. We'll do the first one together.

The French word for *door* is *porte*. I think of a bottle of port hanging from a door.

I'm going to give you the words now:

Door, *porte*		Tablecloth, *nappe*	
Sea, *mer*		Blanket, *couverture*	
Mouth, *bouche*		Menu, *carte*	
Grass, *herbe*		Jacket, *veste*	
Clock, *pendule*		Hen, *poule*	

How were those quick-fire associations? Again, let me give you the French word, and see if you can give me the English equivalent.

Porte	*Nappe*
Mer	*Couverture*
Bouche	*Carte*
Herbe	*Veste*
Pendule	*Poule*

What sort of associations did you come up with? With *sea* and *mer*, I think of a *mayor* of a town swimming in a *sea*. With *mouth* and *bouche*, you can think of a bushy mustache covering someone's mouth. What about a herbal sort of grass for *herbe*? With *clock* and *pendule*, you think of a pendulum. Tablecloth: *napkin* for *nappe*. These words bridge the gap between the English word and its foreign equivalent.

Couverture for *blanket*: you think of *cover*. *Carte*: maybe a playing card on the *menu*. *Jacket*, *veste*, that's a ready-made connection. *Hen* is *poule*. Maybe you think of a hen playing a game of pool or swimming in a pool.

A friend of mine was exasperated with his son because he couldn't learn French, so he asked me to give him some private lessons. The son was really bad at it. He couldn't even tell the difference between the masculine and feminine genders, and he'd been studying the language for two years.

This was his first clue to learning French: I said, "Listen, Dave. The next time you have trouble with *le* and *la*, just think of two people, *Len* and *Laura*. So, now, Dave, is *Len* masculine or feminine?"

"Masculine."

"Great. So is *le* masculine or feminine?"

"It's masculine, of course." You could see a little light switch on in Dave's head. He said, "Ah, so that's a good way of learning French."

By the way, Dave passed his French exam, which totally baffled his French teacher. He didn't get top grades—I got him at the eleventh hour—but he wasn't even expected to take the exam.

Try it for yourself. It's fast, it's a quantum leap in learning languages.

AN INTERPLANETARY TRIP

How about that interplanetary trip that I mentioned? Can you name the order of the planets in our solar system? There are nine, including earth: 4 large and 4 small.

I'm going to give you a story, and I want you to visualize the scenes. Let them wash over you as I go through the story. At the end of it, you should be able to name the planets and tell me if Saturn is large or small.

We'll have the moon as a backdrop for these images. Imagine that you're on a spaceship, and you're slowly descending to the surface of the moon. As you're getting closer, the surface is very hot, so the temperature is rising. You have a little thermometer. What do you have in a thermometer? Mercury. It's a small thermometer, so now you can remember that the first planet from the sun is Mercury.

Your spaceship lands. You open the hatch, and there to greet you is a beautiful little girl. What's her name? Venus. She's a beautiful girl. She's small, because Venus is a small planet.

Venus is very kindly. In case you get homesick, she's given you a big pile of earth just in case you got a bit lonesome, to remind you of Earth. She's dumped this next to your spacecraft, because Earth is the next planet.

On the top of the mound, you see a fiery little man. He's angry because Venus has dumped all this earth on him. He's the god of war, and he's eating a Mars bar. He must be Mars. Why is he a little man? Because Mars is a small planet. It's also the next planet after Earth.

Suddenly you hear this thump, thump, thump, and the ground shakes. You look in the distance on the horizon, and you see the lunar landscape. From behind the mountain, you see this giant, who is Jupiter. He's a giant because Jupiter is a big planet. He's also a sun worshiper. He has a T-shirt on, and you can see the letters S-U-N. That's a clue for the next 3 planets: Saturn, Uranus, and Neptune.

Just from that image, you have encapsulated the planets beyond Jupiter: Saturn, Uranus, and Neptune. So you know they're all big planets.

OK. From the letter N, you see a little lead that goes off into the distance. It's a dog lead. You know what's going to happen next. The lead is attached to a small dog, because it's a small planet. Yes, it's Pluto.

Do you have that story in your head? Let's go back over the story and see if you can get the planets in order. Remember, you're in the spaceship. What's the first planet from the sun? You look at the thermometer. It has to be Mercury, and you know it's a small planet.

Open the hatch: Venus. What has she brought for you? Earth. What comes out of the earth? It has to be Mars. Thump, thump: Jupiter. Look at the T-shirt: Saturn, Uranus, and Neptune. What's attached to the end? It's a lead that goes all the way back to Pluto. Wonderful.

If I ask you, is Saturn a large planet or a small one? it's obvious, isn't it? It has to be a large planet. What comes after Saturn? Uranus. What comes before Saturn? It has to be Jupiter.

You have those ingredients again: imagination, association, and location. All you have to do is think about that story again tomorrow and in about a week's time, and you'll have that information for a long, long time. Wasn't that enjoyable to learn?

The mechanism by which memory works is association. Allow your vibrant, creative imagination to find a link to bridge the gap between a word and its meaning. Look for patterns in words to help with spelling, like the *symmetry* of *cemetery.*

Let your imagination go on an interplanetary trip so you can memorize the planets. Look for links between foreign words and their meanings. The German word for *rain* is *regen.* Simple. What's the link? Imagine lots of Ronald Reagans falling from the sky.

Maybe you're a student where you take regular business trips abroad. Use these techniques to learn vocabulary in a foreign language. This is the lazy man's way of soaking up knowledge. Use these techniques and the power of association and imagination to boost your word power. Become a walking thesaurus. That's quantum memory power working for you at its best.

NUMBER ONE HITS

In the summer of 1993, I had the pleasure of working with a number of well-known presenters and celebrities on a radio road show in England. I was billed as the Memory Man, and the public were invited to test my knowledge of number 1 hits spanning the last 40 years. A random date from those years would be called out, and I was expected to say what was number one on the charts on that day, who the singer was, how many weeks it was number one, and the record label for that particular hit.

For example, if someone shouted out, "What was number 1 on February 21, 1956?" I would say it was "Memories Are Made of This," sung by Dean Martin. It was on the Capitol Records label, and it was number one for 4 weeks.

Unlike my audience at the time, who thought I must be born with unique powers of recall, you should have a pretty good idea of how I was able to memorize so much information. I was, of course, referring to a series of mental journeys and recalled images and scenes from them.

To remember 40 years of number 1 hits, I needed 40 separate journeys, each consisting of about 20 stages, depending on the number of hits for that particular year. The routes I chose were mostly located in and around the beautiful city of Prague in the Czech Republic. I happened to be in Prague on a gambling trip organized by a news-paper, and in between visits to casinos, I would grab a list of two or three years' worth of hits and proceed to explore interesting parts of the city.

As I weaved my way around the streets and parks of Prague, I began translating the details of my pop trivia into rich, mnemonic scenes. I started to superimpose them on suitable stops along the way, much to the bemusement, and in one case the suspicion, of others. I can remember standing at the corner of one street holding a piece of paper and staring at what was probably an old government building. When a middle-aged man approached me and asked me what I was doing, I got the impression that he thought I might be spying. My answer left him with an expression on his face like that of an untipped waiter. "Well," I said, "I'm trying to remember that 'Wooden Heart' was number one on March 23, 1961, and that Elvis Presley sang it." Before I got around to explaining my strange behavior, the man was shaking his head and walking off in disbelief.

When I eventually left Prague, I returned home with both a permanent memory of the layout of that city and a lasting knowledge of 40 years of music.

Here's another quick exercise for you. I'm going to give you some British number one hits from 1961. I'm going to give you 10, so I want you to form a journey, any journey you like this time, and make sure there are 10 stages. So set down the book.

When you're ready, I'm going to give you the song title. If you're old enough, you might remember them. If you don't, just turn the descriptions into a single mnemonic image.

For example, the first one I'm going to give you is "Poetry in Motion." These are all hits from 1961. OK, are you ready?

First stage, use your imagination. Here it comes: "Poetry in Motion." Next stage: "Are You Lonesome Tonight?" Third stage: "Sailor." Fourth stage: "Walk Right Back." Next stage: "Wooden Heart."

Next: "Blue Moon." Next: "On the Rebound." Next stage: "You're Driving Me Crazy." Next: "Surrender." Finally: "Runaway."

Keep thinking all the time. Go back to the first stage. What are you thinking of? Something in motion—"Poetry in Motion." Again, see if you can think of the images before you read the titles: "Poetry in Motion," "Are You Lonesome Tonight?" "Sailor," "Walk Right Back," "Wooden Heart," "Blue Moon," "On the Rebound," "You're Driving Me Crazy," "Surrender," and "Runaway."

How did you get on?

Once you have those songs along your journey and you know them well, you can start connecting the artist to the song. This time, go back over the journey and try to connect the artist to the image that you formed for the song. You'll probably know some of these names. Others will be completely alien to you.

For example, for the first scene that you created, "Poetry in Motion," the artist is Johnny Tillotson. You're going to need all the powers of your imagination here and creativity to connect those—"Poetry in Motion" and Johnny Tillotson.

Now move on to the next stage: Elvis Presley. Next, Petula Clark. Next stage: the Everly Brothers. Next: Elvis Presley again. Next: the Marcels. Next: Floyd Cramer. Next stage: Temperance Seven. Next stage: Elvis Presley yet again. Finally: Del Shannon.

Keep thinking all the time, and let's see if you've connected the artist with the song. Go back again. For "Poetry in Motion," you should have had Johnny Tillotson. "Are You Lonesome Tonight?"— you should know that one: Elvis Presley.

The next one was "Sailor," and the artist was Petula Clark. "Walk Right Back," the Everly Brothers. "Wooden Heart," Elvis Presley. "Blue Moon" was sung by the Marcels.

"On the Rebound," Floyd Cramer. "You're Driving Me Crazy," that was Temperance Seven. "Surrender" was Elvis Presley, and "Runaway," Del Shannon.

FEAR AND COUNTING IN LAS VEGAS

Is it really possible to beat the casino game of blackjack? I'm always being asked this question. Back in 1995, I was the subject of a British documentary called *Fear and Counting in Las Vegas*. For one month, a film crew monitored my progress playing cards in several gambling states in America. The purpose of the documentary was to see whether or not it is possible to use mental skills to beat the casinos at their own game, that is, to make a profit with blackjack.

When I arrived in Biloxi, Mississippi, I met up with "The Bishop" of blackjack, a guy called Arnold Snyder. If anybody understands blackjack, Arnold does. He spent a lifetime studying the game, and apart from being a successful player himself, he's made millions out of selling willing strategies to potential players. From his base in California, he runs the Blackjack Forum, the only forum dedicated to helping professional card players beat the casinos. I asked the Bishop, "Is it possible to beat the casinos at their own game?"

His short answer was yes. I played for 17 days in the States, and my total profit was $9,571. It's not a fortune, but it does represent an annual profit of approximately $150,000.

Soon after I learned to memorize playing cards, it occurred to me that there must be a way of cashing in on my newfound ability. Blackjack seemed like a natural target. Unlike roulette or dice, which are games of pure chance, blackjack involves a degree of skill.

I was already familiar with the game, having lost many more times than I'd ever won. Like many others, I'd always thought that beating the bank was a romantic but ill-conceived notion, the stuff of fiction, and a surefire way of losing even more money. Memorizing multiple packs of playing cards put a different complexion on things.

Today I'm barred from casinos all over Britain, France, and the Czech Republic, and from many across America. One or two will let me in for a drink, but if I get anywhere near the blackjack tables, I'm back out on the street. They know I have a winning strategy, and if I play for long enough, I could break the bank.

I don't want to encourage anybody to take up gambling; there are many other ways of making money. But my approach to blackjack is a good example of what could be achieved with a trained memory.

Before you go rushing off to your nearest casino armed with this chapter, let me issue you a word of warning. Yes, it is possible to beat the game. The trouble is the casinos are only too well aware of this fact and are constantly on their guard for card counters. Winning the game is not the difficult part. The skill is in avoiding the attention and the inevitable tap on the shoulder from the casino pit bosses.

The primary attraction of the game is that people believe it's beatable. Indeed the casinos advertise it as a game of skill. It's ironic, therefore, that if you get too skillful, they'll prevent you from playing it.

100,000 HANDS OF CARDS

The object of blackjack is to beat the dealer. To do this, you must obtain a total that is greater than the dealer's but doesn't exceed 21. The dealer must draw cards totaling a minimum of 17. Whoever is the closest to 21 wins that particular hand. For the player, the skill lies in deciding how many cards he or she should draw relative to the degree of risk.

As is my nature, I wanted to investigate for myself whether or not it was possible to gain an edge over the dealer without initially referring to textbooks on the subject. So I proceeded to deal out thousands of hands analyzing every possible permutation. After six months, I'd studied 100,000 hands.

I never intended to deal so many cards, but once I started, I was overcome with a relentless urge to continue playing and amassing results. The only way to test my theory satisfactorily was to carry out thousands of individual trials.

You may find the thought of devoting so much time to a card game ridiculous or at least excessive. At the time I often wondered what was really keeping me going. I think I know now, and it's quite uncanny.

After I carried out all these experiments, I came across a some articles about the game of bridge. In December 1932, the *London Evening Standard* published a series of five articles by Dr. E. Gordon Reeve on the "Reeveu" system for contract bridge. This system was invented by Reeve himself, and in one of the article he says, "Three years of illness gave me the opportunity to work out the possibilities of scoring game. I dealt 5,000 hands, and each hand was played by all four players, north, south, east, and west, in all the denominations respectively. Thus, the results of 100,000 combinations of hands were tabulated."

It was a strange feeling coming across such a precedent. It was also comforting to know that I wasn't the only person fanatical enough to be lured into the monotonous task of card permutations, but imagine the shiver that went down my spine when I discovered that this man, whom I had never met—he died in 1938—was my grandfather.

In any event, after dealing out about 100,000 hands, I felt I'd gotten to know the heart and soul of blackjack. Every aspect of the game had been dissected and held up to the light. In the process, I developed a basic card counting strategy, and I got it to the point where if I raised my stake at the right time, in other words, if low cards had gone and high cards were due to come out, then I'd get an advantage of about 1 percent, or $1 for every $100 bet. This was just enough to show a profit.

I began by joining as many clubs as I could all over England. Profits were modest to begin with, but there were other perks of the job. I embarked on a pleasant tour of the casinos along the south coast, enjoying what I called "free evenings." My profit would cover the cost of travel, meals, and drinks.

It wasn't long before I was targeting the Midlands and certain London clubs and returning most mornings with a reasonable profit. The strategy was working. More importantly, the casino managers appeared to be tolerating my presence. I began to earn a good living, about $750 to $1,000 a week. I was learning to ride the ups and downs.

I remember getting off to a particularly bad start on my first visit to a club in the Midlands. Within half an hour, I was $750 down. I decided that a good dinner was in order, so after dining on a sumptuous steak washed down with a delightful wine, I was pleasantly surprised to find that my dinner bill had been taken care of by the manager. In the States, this is called *comping*.

The manager had spotted a gambler with potential. Managers do this from time to time to encourage you to gamble more and more money. But I returned to the blackjack table and not only recouped my losses but ended up showing a profit of $750.

I tried to share my delight with the manager, celebrating my change of fortune and thanking him for the delicious dinner. The look on his face signaled the beginning of the end of a beautiful relationship. After two or more similar visits, I was barred.

After a while, I got a bit greedy. This was small reward for a dangerous sort of lifestyle. I sought more and more profit and was soon taking home $1,500 a day. Then I became a marked man.

Word travels fast in the casino world. In England, you have to be a member of a club to get into a casino. Scores of letters began to drop into the letterbox terminating my memberships in casinos nationwide. This is a letter from one London club: "Dear Mr. O'Brien, it is the decision of the committee that your membership be withdrawn from this club. This is effective immediately, and our reception has been advised accordingly. You will also be refused entry to the premises as a guest of a member."

THE SYSTEM

Here's how you get an advantage in blackjack. One third of the time, the game is pretty much level between you and the dealer. A little over one third of the time, the dealer has a slight edge, and just under one third of the time, you have a narrow edge. The beauty of card counting is that it tells you when you have that slight statistical edge, thus enabling you to make bigger bets.

Card counting is an art and a science, much like memory itself, and it requires quite a bit of practice. The richer the proportion of high cards to low cards, the greater your chances of winning. The idea is to keep track of all the cards that have been dealt, so you know what's left in the shoe.

One of the best ways to monitor this flow of highs and lows is to assign specific weights to each card. You can do that by using a simple plus/minus count strategy.

When small cards are removed from the deck, you have the advantage. For every small card you see, count plus 1. Ignore the 7, 8, and 9. These are neutral cards, and they have little effect on the balance of play. As high-value cards are removed, the dealer gains a small edge. So for each high card you see, you count minus 1.

If you get hold of a deck of cards, and you deal through and you count as each card goes through, by the end of the deck, if you've been accurate, then the count should end up at zero.

Whenever you're in a plus count at the gaming table, you're likely to get higher-value cards, balancing the total out to zero. That's when you should increase your stake. This is the essence of card counting, but you'll find it's a bit frowned upon in Las Vegas these days.

Unfortunately, I can't get into any casinos in the U.K. anymore, so these days the only way I can get into a casino is if I take other people in and give them a master class on blackjack. Of course, we don't play for profit; it's just for fun.

THE ACADEMY AWARDS

Time for another fun exercise. This time, I'm going to give you the 9 films that received Academy Awards for Best Picture from 1991 to 1999. So form a journey, doesn't matter where it is, but get a journey of 9 stages. As I read out the descriptions, turn those into memorable, colorful images.

Are you ready? Remember, use the power of association. Use the first thing that comes into you head.

First stage, this is 1991: *The Silence of the Lambs*. Next stage: 1992, *Unforgiven*. Next stage, 1993: *Schindler's List*. Next stage, 1994: *Forrest Gump*. Then, 1995: *Braveheart*. Next stage, 1996: *The English Patient*. In 1997: *Titanic*. Next stage, stage 8: *Shakespeare in Love*. Finally, at the last stage, 1999: *American Beauty*.

Keep thinking all the time. Go back again to the first stage. You should be able to get all these now. In 1991, what was it? You see some lambs: *The Silence of the Lambs*. Next stage, *Unforgiven*. Next, *Schindler's List, Forrest Gump, Braveheart, The English Patient, Titanic, Shakespeare in Love, American Beauty*. Did you get all those?

Now if anybody asks you, "What won the Academy Award for Best Picture in 1995?" you can say, "That was *Braveheart*."

"What was before that, in 1994?" Just think back through your journey: *Forrest Gump*. "How about 1996?" It has to be *The English Patient*.

If you had to memorize that list using traditional methods, like repeating it over and over again, how long do you think that would take? Using quantum memory power techniques, you've done it in just a couple of minutes, so now you're a film buff.

12

The Secret to Remembering Dates

. . . .

n this chapter, I'm going to teach you how to be a walking calendar. If someone gives me their date of birth, I can give them the day of the week they were born in seconds. For example, the 10th of August 1957 was a Saturday, and the 10th of August 2057 will be a Friday, and I'll be exactly 100 years old, should I be so lucky.

For instance, someone might say, "I was born on April 7, 1961." I'd say, "That's a Friday."

"My kid was born on June 27, 1991." That was a Thursday. Being able to tell the day of the week is not just a great party trick, but it's also a great way of settling arguments. "No, you couldn't have been on the optician that day, because that was a Sunday."

Whenever I hear dates in history, I often wonder if the corresponding day of the week had any influence on its occurrence. For example, remember that fateful day on December 8, 1980, when John Lennon was murdered. I know immediately that it was a Monday. I wonder if Mark David Chapman, his killer, had the Monday blues.

Do you remember the moon landing on July 20, 1969? I can remember as a kid. I was about 11 years old, staying up all night with my mother watching it. Now I can remember that it was a Sunday, but I could also work it out through my system.

How about some more famous date? If you're old enough, you can probably remember what you were doing on November 22, 1963, the day Kennedy was shot. I know immediately that it was a Friday.

By the end of this chapter, you'll be able to work these calculations out for yourself, because I'm going to let you into a secret that psychic mind performers and magicians would rather I didn't reveal. The skill involves about 75 percent memory and 25 percent math. What takes several sentences for me to explain could be calculated by your brain in a second—with a little bit of practice, of course.

Before I give you this method, just bear in mind the example of a pianist. Watch a pianist at work, sight-reading a score. Do you think he really has time to convert what he sees on a score and translate it into notes on a piano? No, he doesn't. He just knows where his fingers should go. It's automatic after a while, and it's a bit like watching somebody typing. If you've never seen it before, you'd have thought it was impossible. How can your brain work out something so quickly?

What I'm about to explain is a lot easier than that. It's a lot less involved than trying to learn sight-reading from scratch. It might sound a bit complicated, but it isn't really. So how do I do this? How do I do it so quickly?

You can do it too. I'm going to give you a few examples, and I'm going to talk broadly about how it's possible. I have a series of codes, so that every year to me represents a single-digit code. When I hear the year 1957, I immediately think of the code 1. If it's 1963, that's 1 as well; 1953, I get the code 3; 1999, the code 4. I'm going to tell you how to memorize those codes in a minute.

The next thing you need is a separate code for each month. When I hear February, I immediately think of the code 4. December is 6. April is 0.

The third thing is, you have to know a symbol for each day of the week. That's simple. Sunday is always the first day of the week, so Monday is 2, Tuesday 3, Wednesday 4, and so on. I end with Saturday.

With this particular technique, I just cancel out anything that's divisible by 7. On this basis, Saturday should be 7, but I'm going to call it 0. It's divisible by 7, and that works with the date as well. So if you have the 7th of the month, you call that 0. If it's the 22nd, you take away the multiples of 7—3 7s—and that leaves you with 1.

Let me go through this step by step. Let's take that date again, my birthday, August 10, 1957. The code for August is 3, so keep that in mind: 3. Now we take the date: the 10th. Take away the 7, and that leaves 3. Now we have August 3, and the date, 3. One more code coming up.

For 1957, the code is 1. You add those 3 together: 3 plus 3 is 6, plus the 1 is 7. What do you do? You cancel out the 7, so we're left with 0. What is 0? It's Saturday.

You must always remember that what takes me several sentences to describe can be worked out by your brain in seconds. Of course, you need a bit of practice. You need to learn the codes.

MONTH CODES

Let's start off with the month codes, and this will act as a little exercise for you. There are only 12 codes to learn, starting with January and going right through to December.

January is 1, so how can you find a link between January and 1? That's an easy one. It's the first month, so the code is 1.

Let's go on to February, which is 4. Think of the Fab 4, the Beatles: Fab 4, Feb. 4.

For March, think of an army marching forward, because the code for March is also 4. Use images; use your imagination.

The code for April is 0. For that, I imagine April showers, and I can see hailstones the size of footballs. Remember the number shape for 0 is a football. Just visualize that now.

What about May? I may think of May, or I may not. It's a twofold choice, and the code for May is 2.

The code for June is 5. How would you find a link between June and 5? I think of a friend of mine called June drawing her curtains. Remember the number shape for 5 is a curtain hook. Maybe you know somebody called June. Just imagine her at home pulling her curtains, and you'll always remember that the code for June is 5. It's best to use your own associations. You could think of June Cleaver from the old TV show *Leave It to Beaver*. Imagine her pulling the curtains.

The code for July is 0. Again, use the number shape. Imagine somebody you know called Julie kicking a football.

Now we move on to August. The code for August is 3. How would you find a connection between August and 3? I think of the star sign Leo, which has 3 letters. Does that make sense? August 3, Leo 3.

We can use something similar with September. I think of September—the fall, leaves falling, and *leaves* has 6 letters, so September is 6. September, leaves, 6.

We're nearly there. October makes me think of an *octopus*. The code is 1. How do you connect *octopus* with a *candle*, which is the number shape for 1? Picture an octopus carrying a candle.

November is 4. What's the first thing that comes into your mind when you hear November? I think of a *novice*, a Franciscan friar. The number shape for 4 is a sailboat, so just imagine a novice on the serene sea. Perhaps he's reading a Bible, and he's in a sailboat drifting out to sea. *November, novice, sailboat, 4.*

I'm going to leave the last one up to you. The code for December is 6. See if you can find a connection between December and 6.

Now for the test. I'm going to go back through those months, and I want you to give the code.

January: the clue is, it's the first month, 1.

For February, think of the Beatles, the Fab 4.

March, an army marching forward. March is 4.

April—April showers, hailstones the size of footballs, so April is 0.

May, may or may not—a twofold choice. May is 2.

June: who was that woman? What was she doing? She was drawing the curtains, and the number shape for 5, that's it: curtain hook. June is 5.

July, or Julie. What was Julie doing? Kicking a football, so 0 is the number code for July.

What was the association for August? The star sign Leo. Leo has 3 letters, so it's 3.

September is the beginning of the fall. Falling leaves, and *leaves* has how many letters? 6.

For October, we thought of what? An octopus carrying a candle: number shape 1.

For November, what was that serene scene? The novice in the sailboat: 4.

I don't know what you were thinking of, but the number for December is 6.

Now that you have the month codes, let's go back to that date again: August 10, 1957. If I give you the code for 1957, it's 1. You should be able to work it out for yourself now. August 10, take away the 7, and that leaves 3. What is the code for August? 3, so 3 plus 3 plus 1 gives us Saturday. It'll become clearer later on.

YEAR CODES

Now we come to the year codes. As I said, every pair of digits from 00 to 99 is a person to me. When I hear 57, I think of my friend, Theresa. Now I know the number code is 1, but how do I do that?

I want you to imagine this. It's your birthday. You're walking up your drive, you're just about to go in the front door, and you're thinking, "What should I do tonight? Maybe I'll invite some friends around for drinks and have an early night."

As you open the door, an almighty cheer reverberates around the house. Little did you know that your best friend has organized a huge party for you. He's invited 100 guests, so as the light goes on, you see your friends and family, but as you look around, you notice famous people, sports personalities, politicians, royalty, even people from the past.

Of course, you can't fit 100 guests into one room, so your friend has designated various rooms for groups of people. In fact, he's designated 7 areas, including the yard, so the yard is one area, and he has various people in little cliques. You know how people gather in cliques. Some gather in the kitchen, some in the sitting room.

This is how you learn the year codes. You imagine all 100 year codes being split up into 7 areas. Let me give you an example.

The area in the garden we'll call the code area of 0. Now, there you have characters like Omar Sharif, the cartoon character Olive Oyl, and Benny Hill. If you link those back to numbers, you have Omar Sharif, OS being 06. Remember the Dominic system? What would Olive Oyl be? 00. It has to be OO, 00. Benny Hill (or Bob Hope): BH. He has to be 28.

What's happening in your bedroom? You have Alfred Hitchcock there, along with Neil Armstrong and Sean Connery.

If this were your own house, and you had 100 famous people there, do you think that after the party you'd be able to remember where everybody was situated? Of course you would, because you'd want to keep an eye on them. You'd want to make sure that they have drinks and that they're not up to no good.

Splitting your own house up into 7 areas is a really fun way of exercising your brain. It's also an extremely useful, beneficial, and practical technique to have.

HOW IT WORKS

To demonstrate how this works, we're going to take a few of those guests and put them in the yard. Think about your own yard, and form a little journey of seven stages around it. At each stage, you're going to imagine seeing some famous characters, and they're going to be kicking a football to one another. Remember, the number shape for 0 is football, and that's why we have it in the yard. That will give you the number code for each of the following years.

When you have 7 stages, I'm going to feed you the images of famous people or cartoon characters. Try to picture these characters.

First one: Olive Oyl, Omar Sharif, Alec Guinness. Imagine him drinking Guinness: Alec Guinness. Bing Crosby, Benny Hill, Celine Dion, and Duke Ellington.

Can you picture those characters in your yard? Try to get them to interact with each other. They're kicking a football around. That will remind you that the code is 0.

If you think about those characters, you can work back to the year dates. Olive Oyl will be OO, 00: 1900. Omar Sharif is going to be 06, 1906. Alec Guinness, AG, will be 1917. Bing Crosby, 1923; Benny Hill, 1928: Celine Dion, CD, 1934; and Duke Ellington, 1945.

We take any one of those dates, and now we're going to work out the day of the week together. May: what's the code for May? It's 2. Keep this in your head. May 3, so now you had 2 plus 3, and you have 5: 1906. Who is 06? It has to be Omar Sharif. He's in the garden. The code is 0, so you're still on 5. What's the fifth day of the week? Sunday, Monday, Tuesday, Wednesday, Thursday.

As I said before, it takes a while to learn this, and it takes a while to explain it, but with a bit of practice, you'll be able to do it in seconds.

A TEST

Here's another one for you. When people give me dates, I try to get them to give me the year first, so I have the code. Let's say the first year you get is 1900, so you're looking at OO, 00, which is Olive Oyl. We can discount the year now, because we know she's in the garden, and the code is 0, so now we just get straight on to the actual date itself. August 3: 3 plus 3 is 6. What does that give us? Friday.

One more for you. We'll do it the other way around. December: code 6, December 21. Remember you cast out the 7s, so with 21 divided by 7, you're left with 0. December is 6; Then there's 1906. Now you think, who is 06? That's Omar Sharif; he's in the garden, 0, so we're still on 6. It has to be Friday, the sixth day of the week.

As I said, take a bit of time to learn this process. Go over it, and it should all make sense. If you want to get really clever, you can do this for almost any century you like. You can go backwards or forwards. All you have to do is learn another set of codes for the centuries.

Now a word on the leap year. There is going to be a slight adjustment for any date that comes in January or February. A leap year is any year that's divisible by 4. So 1944 is an obvious one, as is 1972, so when you get a leap year, have a look at the guidebook. It's a very simple, slight adjustment. Let us suppose the date you are asked about is a leap year and falls between 1 January and 29 February. In this case (and no other), simply subtract 1 from your final total. If the date falls within a leap year, but is outside January or February, simply carry out the calculation as before.

This is a great skill to have, and you can have a lot of fun with it. You'll be known as a walking calendar. If you think it's rather difficult, my mother, who is 83, can do it. She's not as fast as I am, but she always gets it right.

In the next chapter, we're going to look at ways of developing the photographic side of your memory. We're also going to be looking at ways of remembering directions.

13

A Frame of Reference

. . . .

In this chapter, we're going to look at how you can develop your powers of photographic memory. In fact, most of us already possess a degree of photographic memory.

My father told me a story about when he was 10. He was sitting on a train with his parents, traveling across Ireland from Dublin, and he decided to try and capture that moment. He just took in all the information. He studied the expressions on his parents' faces as well as their clothes. He looked around at the decor of the train, noted that special musty smell that only trains give off, and looked at the scenery outside as well.

"That's it," he said. "I'm going to keep that memory in my mind for life." He said he could still remember it to that day. I thought it was such a lovely, elegant idea that I decided to do it myself in the exact instant my father told me the story.

Guess where we were sitting? I was age 12, and we were also sitting on a train traveling across Ireland from Dublin.

Maybe you have a moment like that in your lifetime. Perhaps you can remember walking up the aisle at your wedding, or your first day at school. How many details can you recall?

If we can remember information in detail, like a specific framed moment in our past, why shouldn't we able to memorize the contents of a newspaper or a magazine?

I regularly give presentations, and I do the usual things. I talk about memory training, and then we get on to memorizing a number. I recall everybody's names, and we do a deck of cards. But I think the one thing that baffles most people is when I get that day's newspaper out and memorize it. I'll ask somebody to give me any page; say they choose page 67. I'll say, "On that particular page, there's probably an advert, and it's all about PCs," and then I'll reel off the specifications, the price, and the telephone number for more information.

Somebody else will shout out another page, and I'll say, "There's a picture there of six people," and then I'll recall their names. Maybe there's a car in the background, so I'll reel off the number on the license plate.

This goes on for a bit, and eventually somebody will pick out the financial section. I'll say, "No problem. Somebody call out a company."

They'll say, "How about CJ Holdings?"

"That went up 67.75 cents. Another."

"Tech Back stock," or whatever it is.

I'll say, "Yes, that went down, I think that was $12.50." At the end of this (if I'm paid enough money), I'll actually remember the exact price: it moved down, say $10 to $3.53.

How do I do that? If you apply the techniques that I'm about to give you, you can do this too. It's not that difficult.

A quick revision. What are the three golden keys of memory? *Association*, *location*, and *imagination*. Just think of Muhammad Ali, ALI, "The Greatest," because these are the greatest components for converting a poor memory into a mammoth memory.

A JOURNEY THROUGH THE NEWSPAPER

This is what I normally do. The first thing, as always, is to get myself a location. I usually choose one out in the open air.

Do you remember when we did a shopping list?
I got you to go on a journey around your house.
The areas there were probably a little confined.
That's fine, because you're only looking at doing
one object in one room, but when you're looking at
a newspaper, you need a wide expanse. So the journey I want you to choose now is a favorite walk,
such as a walk through the park.

I prepare the journey; let's say the first stage
is the front gate or the entrance to the park. The
second one might be a tree, an interesting tree,
that you can use as a second stage. The third stage
might be a children's play area.

Then I just flick through the newspaper and
pick out the central themes. Say I see Madonna
on the front page, so she's at the first stage of the
journey.

Then I go to the next page, and I look for anything that grabs my eye. Say it's "Widow Wins
Lottery," so I picture a widow at the second stage
of the journey, by the tree.

Then I go to the third page and see an advert
for mobile phones. Again, I associate that theme,
the mobile phone, with the location, which is the
children's play area.

Then I have a quick run-through. I think, "Who
was at the front gate?" Madonna. She had running

shoes on; maybe she's going for a run in the park.
I go to stage 2; there's a tree there. What was it?
Oh, yes, the caption, "Widow Wins Lottery." Then
I go to stage 3, the children's play area. Maybe
there's a kid at the top of the slide, and he has a
mobile phone, and so on.

Once I have that, then I have hangers or hooks
to which I can now attach more and more information. Have you noticed that when you read a newspaper, although a lot of the information goes in,
sometimes you forget a lot of it because you don't
know how to access it? It's not until you go down
to the bar and someone says, "Did you hear about
that widow?" that you remember. You say, "Oh,
yes. She's the one who won all those millions," and
then all the information comes out. The beauty
about the journey system is that it allows you to
access all the information in order.

Go back to the first stage again. This time, look
at more details about Madonna, and add those in.
It might be that it's her 41st birthday, so if you
want to remember that, use the Dominic system:
41 translates to DA, which gives you Dan Aykroyd.
So put him in the scene with Madonna.

Then you go to the next page, with some more
information about the widow, and you keep building up your knowledge all the time.

A NEWSPAPER EXERCISE

We're going to do an exercise now, and we're going to simulate memorizing the contents of a newspaper, but we're only going to do 10 pages.

Form a journey in the open air. It could be around a park or a favorite walk of yours, a journey of 10 stages. Once you have the stages, you can read abut the images I will give you.

As you do, try to connect each of these images to the specific location. Go to the first location in your mind's eye now, and I'm going to give you the first image. Here we go.

It's an aircraft. Just use all your senses: touch, taste, sight, smell, sound, emotion, color, movement. Anchor that to the background: aircraft.

Now go to the next stage, stage 2. This time you see a photograph or a poster of the actor James Dean. See if you can conjure up that image. Now anchor him to your background.

At the next stage, stage 3, I want you to picture a typical summer scene. It's on a river, and there are some boats there. Got that?

Move on to stage 4. This time it's an advert for a pair of socks, so how would you connect that to the scene, to your geography? Use logic.

OK, moving on. You're on your walk now. You're halfway through, at stage 5. This time I want you to picture the photograph of a telephone booth.

At stage 6 is a typical scene that you might see in a park. Some children are playing soccer.

Moving on now, to stage 7, picture this: 2 50-cent pieces.

Go onto the next stage, stage 8. This time it's another poster. It's a poster for the film *Jaws*.

At the next stage, stage 9, is a photograph of a gift shop. How would you connect that to the background?

Finally, at stage 10, you see a pair of mailboxes.

Keep reviewing all the time. Go back to the very first stage again, so you're back at the first stage. What do you see? Aircraft. Next stage: a poster of James Dean. Third stage: a boating scene on the river. Keep going to stage 4: an advert for a pair of socks.

Stage 5 is the telephone box.

At the next stage, stage 6, some kids are playing soccer.

Then we have a pair of 50-cent pieces; then a poster for the film *Jaws*. Then it was the gift shop, and finally a pair of mailboxes. OK, you have that in your head now.

USING HANGERS AND HOOKS

Now the trick is to attach more information using hangers or hooks. Go back to the first stage. You have the aircraft. We're going to start filling in some details, using all the techniques that I've given you before, such as number shapes. I want you to convert the information into images and attach them to each of your symbols that you have in the picture.

I'll go through the first one with you. Remember, you have an aircraft in your scene. Here's a flight number I want you to convert into another image and attach to that aircraft. The flight number is AA91. Think about it. How are you going to split those up and convert them into images?

Well, you can think of American Airlines, or you can think of Andre Agassi. What about 91? Well, that converts into NA in the Dominic system, which gives you the astronaut Neil Armstrong. Andre Agassi and Neil Armstrong: AA91. Got the picture?

Move on to the next stage. It's that poster of James Dean, and the caption underneath it says, "Rebel without a Cause." You probably know that like the back of your hand anyway, so I want you to bring that to life: "Rebel without a Cause." Remember that pose where he has a leather jacket on and a cigarette?

Moving on to stage 3 now: it's that summer scene with the boats. The caption is, "Temperature Soars to 88 Degrees." Again you have to convert the numbers into pictures, so 88, using the Dominic system, would give us HH. Who's your character for HH? How about Hulk Hogan? Have him in the boat now. Again, immerse yourself in the picture.

Moving on now to stage 4, which was an advert for a pair of socks. We have a price tag here: $6. You could convert 6 into, say, an elephant's trunk, so you connect the elephant to the socks.

Next stage is the telephone booth. There's a note saying that you have to phone this number: extension 189. You split that into a pair of digits. It gives you a person: Alfred Hitchcock, 18. Then you have the 9, for which the number shape is a balloon and string. So you have Alfred Hitchcock holding a balloon and string, and he's by the telephone booth.

Moving on to that soccer game: the caption is, "The Score Is 7–3." Again, you just convert those into letters: 7–3 gives you GC, which gives you George Clooney. Have him playing soccer with the kids.

Next stage. It's those 50-cent pieces. The caption is, "Metal Detector Finds Treasure of 50-Cent Pieces." Imagine yourself there with a metal detector, and you've come across a treasure of 50-cent pieces.

Stage 8 is that poster of *Jaws*. Remember that famous poster? The caption is, "Dentists on Strike." I'll leave that one up to you.

The second to the last stage is the gift shop, and look at the photograph in your mind's eye. The name of the shop is Present Company.

Finally, it's those 2 mailboxes, and the caption is, "Scientists Clone Mailbox."

Just go over the scenes again, review the scenes, let them wash over you, and see what information comes to the fore.

Go back again, what do you see at stage 1? It's an aircraft, flight number AA91. Next stage: James Dean; caption, "Rebel without a Cause." Easy one. Stage 3: that boating scene, and the caption was, "Temperature Soars to—" think of it: Hulk Hogan. It has to be 88 degrees.

Next stage: it's an ad for a pair of socks, and the price is—think of the elephant—$6. It's easy, isn't it?

Next stage is the telephone box. What's the extension number? Just think of Alfred Hitchcock with a balloon and string. It has to be 189.

Next stage is the football game. Who's there? The actor George Clooney: that's GC, which gives you 73, so that's the score: 7–3.

For stage 7, what's the caption? "Metal Detector Finds Treasure of 50-Cent Pieces."

Now comes the famous poster of *Jaws,* and what's the caption? "Dentists on Strike."

Next stage is the gift shop, and what's it called? What's the title above the shop? Present Company.

Finally, it's those two mailboxes, so the caption is, "Scientists Clone Mailbox."

Can you see how it's working, how the initial symbolic images are acting as coat hangers? They're hooks, so you can attach more and more information. If you go back again and add more information to the new images that you're creating all the time, that's the basis on which you can memorize the entire contents of a newspaper. Obviously the speed comes with practice, and if you really take it to the nth degree, you can end up memorizing the day's stock market.

REMEMBERING DIRECTIONS

Now we're going to look at how to remember those directions. I wonder if this has happened to you before: You're driving through a town. You're already five minutes late for a very important meeting. The signs are terrible, and so are the directions you were given. In desperation you wind down the window, and you say to a passerby,

"I'm in a terrible hurry. I have to get to the Lodge Motel."

The guy says, "Oh, I know what that is. You see that road over there? That leads to Grant Avenue, where there's an old Baptist church. Well, you don't want to go down there." You're already late, and this guy's making you even more late.

Eventually he comes out with the right directions: "Turn right into Blue Street. Then you go left into Dolphin Street; take the second exit on the roundabout. Now you'll pass the chocolate factory on the left. Take the fourth turn on the right, and down there, by the satellite center, is the Lodge Motel."

You wind down the window, say, "Thanks very much," only to drive down to the road where the Baptist church is, which is exactly where you were told not to go.

Next time you listen to directions, just feed the information into your brain piece by piece, and use the journey method to lay down the directions.

I'm going to go through those same directions again, but this time we're going to use a route with 6 stages to anchor the images you're about to create. If you live in a city, you could use the layout of streets and avenues to simulate the directions, but for this example, we'll use a golf course.

Picture this with me. We're standing together on the first tee of my local golf course. Now we'll listen to the first direction: turn right into Blue Street. If the direction is to turn right, that's what we're going to do now. We look to our right, and I know that on the first tee of my golf course, there's a tree. What are we going to do? We're going to turn it blue. So imagine a blue tree on the first tee.

Now we walk along to the next stage. We're walking down the first fairway, and now we're taking the next direction: turn left into Dolphin Street. OK, we're told to turn left, so we look to our left, and what do we imagine? We see a dolphin on the first fairway.

Now we come up to the first green. Let's get the next direction in our heads: second exit off the roundabout. This is rather convenient, because we're on a green, which is a round area. If it's the second exit, then I think of the number shape *swan*, 2, so I picture a swan putting on the green.

Now we go to the next stage, which is the second tee. The direction here is to pass the chocolate factory on your left. Again we look at the position to our left. There could be a small marker there, or a hut, so we imagine it made of chocolate. Using more of your imagination now, pass the chocolate factory on your left.

Keep walking. We're at the second fairway now. Next direction: fourth turn on your right. So we look to the right again. Now I know that on the second fairway, there's a big bunker, because I'm always in there. The fourth turning, 4, gives us the number shape *sailboat*, so there's a little sailboat in the bunker.

Now we're at the second green, and we've reached our destination. Down there, by the satellite center, is the Lodge Motel. Imagine a satellite on the green, and you know you've reached your destination.

All you have to do now is review the scene again. Go back to the first tee. What were we told to do? Look to the right, and we see a blue tree. We know we're going to turn right, and the direction is Blue Street. Move down the fairway. This time, what do we see? There's a dolphin, isn't there? Whereabouts is it? It's on the left. That's the direction. Turn left into Dolphin Street.

OK, we're on the first green. What's on the green? What's putting there? It's a swan, isn't it? That's the number shape for 2, so it has to be the second exit on the roundabout.

Now we go to the second tee, and there was something on the left, wasn't there? It was a hut, and it was made of chocolate. The directions were to pass the chocolate factory on your left.

We get on the second fairway. There was something on the bunker, wasn't there, on the right? It was a sailboat. Now we know it's the fourth turn on the right.

Finally, on the second green, we see what? A satellite dish. Ah, now, that's what he said: right next to the satellite center, that's the Lodge Motel.

You can see how this method works. It really is great, because any directions involving a right turn means that I plant a key image to my right. I use number shapes for numbers, as well as movement, color, taste, exaggeration, and so on.

The next time you're lost, take a deep breath and rest assured that your memory won't let you down. Translate those instructions into colorful, symbolic images. Why don't you try this the next time you go on a long journey? By all means take that piece of paper with you, but it's not always practical or safe to keep looking down at it for directions. Try memorizing the information first using the journey method, and see how far you can get. You should get the whole way.

Try this method, and have faith in the incredible power of your memory that by now I hope you're starting to unleash.

14

A Look Inside Your Brain

. . . .

hope that by now you're using these techniques to help you in everyday life. Maybe you've had success in remembering names and faces or in memorizing a shopping list, or maybe you're a student and you've taken advantage of these strategies to speed up learning.

Perhaps you've already impressed your work colleagues by delivering a crisp, unfaltering presentation. They're beginning to ask questions like, "What's happened to you? How come your memory is so efficient?" Are people starting to get suspicious? "Have you been attending some kind of memory course on the quiet?" Or are they simply saying, "How did you do that?"

Have you started to notice something else? Like, are you slightly pleased with yourself, or are you quicker at making connections? Are you able to memorize more and more? Is your imagination getting more creative? Do you feel that you're able to concentrate slightly better? Are you becoming more observant? Are you gaining more confidence in your ability to memorize and recall information? Are you more organized mentally? Maybe you're coping better under pressure. Stress levels are down. Is the metaphor of developing memory muscles making sense to you?

Are your dreams more vivid because you're exercising the visual part of your imagination? Is the quality of your sleep that much better?

At this point we're going to take a look at what's going on in our brains and why memory training is one of the best exercises you can give your mind to develop the whole of your brain.

What are the functions of your left and right brains? Why do you have to be in a certain mood to maximize your concentration? What exactly are the perfect conditions for learning?

If you're not sure whether you're doing these exercises the right way, I'm going to explain in greater depth what it feels like to have a pumped-up memory, what it takes to absorb, say, a 400-digit number in just minutes. I'm going to tell you what it's like to become a memory champion. You are a potential memory champion in your own right, if you want to be.

Why should trying to picture Bing Crosby wearing white flared trousers be good for our brains? I believe that memory training, as described in this book, balances your brain, promoting harmony in all areas of life. It can lead to successful relationships, and yes, to success in business.

To give you my reasons, let's take a little look inside your brain, particularly at the functions of the left and right brain. Your brain, or the upper part of your brain, is known is the *cerebrum*, and it's divided into two parts or sides: the left and right hemispheres. Your brain is essentially a mixture of electricity and chemistry. There's a continuous flow of electricity across the left and the right hemispheres, which varies in frequency throughout the day.

For most of us, the speed at which one side of our brain is operating pretty well matches the speed of the other side; hence the phrase a balanced brain. However, if one side gets damaged, it can lead to an imbalance of brain wave frequency.

Extreme cases, like a stroke, can kill areas of the brain through a lack of oxygen, causing speech loss, or, if speech is maintained, people may feel as though a huge section of their vocabulary has been taken away, like missing pages of a thesaurus.

LEFT AND RIGHT BRAIN FUNCTIONS

Each hemisphere processes information in a slightly different way. The left brain specializes more in serial processing and analyzing information in a linear way—one piece after the other. That's why our left brains are ideally suited to taking in speech, solving problems in a logical way, and dealing with numbers.

The right brain specializes in parallel processing—in other words, taking in several bits of information at the same time. The right brain is better suited for processing pictures, colors, features, and emotions. It's highly active during dreaming.

Generally, the left hemisphere is better suited for things like words, numbers, order, analysis, speech, linear sequence, and logic, whereas the right brain has more to do with spatial awareness, color, dreaming, overview, rhythm, dimension, and of course imagination.

I don't want to give the impression that both sides are isolated, but have you noticed that some people seem to be more inclined one way or the other? You might, for instance, say that someone left-brained, using logic, sequence, numbers, and words, could be an accountant or a lawyer. What about the right brain? Maybe an artist, musician, architect, or dreamer.

Wouldn't it be desirable to develop and engage both hemispheres, to be a good all-arounder, to have a powerful, balanced unison of both sides of your brain, like Leonardo da Vinci?

Bearing in mind these skills of the left and right brain, think for a moment about which side of your brain you're using to memorize a shopping list using the journey method. You're using order throughout the journey, so that's the left brain. Of course, you're using your imagination, so that's the right brain.

You're using spatial awareness: right brain again. What about words? Yes, you're reading words and converting the words from the left brain into pictures in the right brain. You're using color: right brain. You're using logic—remember, I keep telling you to use logic. Make the journey logical, and use logic. Why is Madonna standing at the park gate? Give her a reason, so you're using left brain logic.

You're using overview. You're using serial processing. You're taking information one bit at a time. You're using parallel processing. You're converting serially delivered information and putting that into an overall scene using many things at once.

In fact, you should find you're exercising all of those brain functions. In other words, you're engaging both sides of your brain.

How would these perfectly synchronized hemispheres manifest themselves? What might you expect by blending them? How about colorful logic, imaginative speech, spatial analysis?

Now answer me this. After the first couple of exercises, did you feel that your brain was a little bit strained, a little bit overworked? Like any underused muscle, it takes a while to develop and loosen up.

Was it slightly uncomfortable to begin with doing everything at once—to remember the stages of the journey, to think of an association, to turn it into an image, then exaggerate it and anchor it to the mental background?

Of course it wasn't easy to begin with. You're summoning the whole of your brain. You're asking for the whole of your brain to give you its undivided attention.

If you drive a car, can you remember the first time you had a driving lesson? There were so many things you had to do at once. You had to put your foot on the clutch, into gear, apply your foot to the gas pedal, ease it off, watch the mirror, signal, and maneuver.

Didn't that hurt your head? It hurt mine. Didn't you think to yourself, "I'm never going to master all this. It's just too much to do"? But you did. Driving now is automatic for you.

I believe that this style of memory training will make the act of engaging both sides of your brain become automatic. By doing simple exercises every day, you'll be doing the equivalent of early morning push-ups, just like an athlete who prepares to run by stretching, exercising, and preparing the body. You're preparing your mind, warming it up to deal with the day's events and pressures.

THE 4 TYPES OF BRAIN WAVES

There's more evidence for the balancing, harmonious effect of memory training. Let's look at your brain waves. We use 4 types of brain waves: beta, theta, alpha, and delta. Beta is the fastest. If you're having an epileptic fit, then you're in very high beta, and you're above 30 cycles a second.

When I'm talking, I'm in beta, so in order for me to engage my thoughts and get the words out, my brain has to be operating around about 14 cycles a second. Hopefully, if you're reading, you should be working around about half that speed, and you should be down around alpha, which is about 8 to 10 cycles a second. Alpha is for perfect concentration and for receiving information.

Every so often your brain will slow down even more, down to theta, and theta is the memory wave. This is where you download information. When you're going through the journey, recalling information, and picking up old memories, your brain should be dropping to around about 4 to 7 cycles a second.

When you're dreaming, you're also down in theta. You're having all those lovely dreams, you're seeing images and pictures, and you're this grand film director. You're down around about 3 to 5 cycles a second.

If you drop down to 1 cycle a second, that's delta. That's the lowest level you can reach, and you're not even dreaming then. There's just enough brain wave activity to drive your vital organs.

Throughout the day, we go up and down like a yo-yo. We're using our brain waves in automatic. In order to concentrate, I need alpha and theta rhythms.

Why am I telling you this? Several years ago, I had the opportunity to have my brain waves recorded as I was memorizing a deck of cards, and the results were highly revealing. A few wires were attached to my head with electrodes. Armed with a deck of cards, I thumbed through 52 shuffled cards as I memorized the order in about a minute. Then I named every card in the exact order.

Afterwards I was able to replay the EEG to see how fast or slowly my brain had been working. I used to think that people who could do things like this must have very fast brains, but as I saw from the EEG, my brain waves had actually slowed down, and I was working on a combination of alpha and theta waves.

As I was dealing the cards, I was receiving the information, so I needed to be fairly quiet, down at the alpha wave, about 7 cycles a second, but every so often, I would need to download the memory of the sequence of the cards, so I needed to be in theta as well.

Here's the extraordinary thing: when we played back the EEG from when I recalled the cards, there was no visible alpha, but I had 52 separate theta peaks. In other words, every time I had a memory of a card, it showed up on the screen. For me that was proof that I had to slow my brain down to remember information—right the way down to somewhere between 3 and 5 cycles a second.

PEAK LEARNING WAVES

All this tells us a number of things. To learn at speed, you need to slow down your brain waves, which is a bit of an oxymoron. In any case, it's not a good idea to be shouting or having an argument or being involved in a drama or getting hysterical if you want to study.

It seems that the peak learning wave is the alpha wave. Ideally you want to be in a quiet room with no distractions—somewhere where you can be relaxed. If you want to recall information, you need to slow down even more, to the theta wave.

Think about it. You're more likely to remember events from the past if you're sitting in a quiet room with your eyes shut than you are in the middle of a riot.

By exercising your brain in this manner with any of the practices in this book, you're promoting balance and harmony. As mentioned, you brain has approximately 86 billion neurons, which are its working parts. The combinations of connections between these brain cells give rise to memory.

Every time you have a unique new thought, you're making new connections between neurons in your brain. It's estimated that we use barely 1 percent of our brain's true potential. That's a huge untapped resource.

One question I'm always asked is, don't all those numbers and playing cards just fill up your head? Actually, the more I memorize, the more space I seem to make available for storing new information.

It's amazing. You can actually grow your brain just by thinking new thoughts. New thoughts mean new connections, new pathways in your brain. Thus you have many more ways of solving problems.

When you think of a blue tree standing on the right of the first tee at your local golf course, you're making a brand-new pathway in your brain. Later on, you can use that new pathway to solve a problem. Think about it as a road leading from your house to the airport. If there's only one road, and it gets congested, then you're stuck. But if you have new pathways, you have alternatives; you have many different ways to get to your destination.

That's what's going on in the brain every time you exercise it. That's why I keep saying that not only are these exercises extremely practical, but they're highly beneficial for exercising the whole of your brain.

Why do we admire a quick wit? What is it about comedians that we find attractive? Why do people enjoy exhibiting humor? Perhaps it's because humor indicates a rich mixture of connections in their brains. A politician who can display humor in a timely retort to a difficult or probing question is a vote winner. This politician has an answer for everything. A creative mind is a powerful mind.

GETTING IN THE RIGHT FRAME OF MIND

Here's a meditative exercise for getting in the right frame of mine. You can read these directions in full and practice them afterward, have someone read them to you, or record yourself and listen to the recording as you do this exercise.

Lie down on your back, or sit comfortably in an armchair. With your eyes closed, focus your attention on every muscle in your body, starting with your feet. As you work your way up, let go of any tension in those muscles until your whole body feels like a heavy weight. Start with your toes, and work your way up—every muscle in your body. Feel the tension go as you work your way up.

When you get up to your face, just feel the face muscles, release the tension in them, and let your jaw sag as it succumbs to gravity.

Now, with the rest of your body taken care of, you can concentrate on your breathing. Think about your heartbeat and any feelings of nausea that may be caused by anxiety or stress.

Breathe deeply and slowly, even though your heart might be pumping away furiously. Using your imagination, translate whatever feelings of pain and nausea you may have into an associative, tangible images.

For example, I feel the occasional sensation of nausea at the back of my throat, which I picture as a slow trickle of tiny, grayish pellets. Lower down, in my chest, they gather into a heaving mass of sticky, soot-covered ball bearings.

Whatever representations you make of your tensions or discomforts, imagine a hand dipping into your body, grabbing the offending objects, and throwing them miles away. Continue the process until the stress has been removed.

With your body relaxed, you're breathing deeply, and your nausea is reduced, conjure up an image of a place or a person that gives you thoughts of peace, maybe a happy or relaxed feeling. This could be a scene from your childhood, a holiday location, or a loved one. Latch on to that image, and try to immerse yourself in those pleasant, warm feelings.

Slowly superimpose that pleasant picture onto the image of your anxiety. You might, for example, visualize walking into the examination room in college or the boardroom at work and seeing your loved ones standing there.

In my case, I use the scene of a quiet casino with a croupier standing at an empty blackjack table. That always gives me a good feeling. Sitting on the table is not a deck of playing cards, but a word processor, which normally represents work, deadlines, accounts, and other aspects of responsibility. By blending or mixing the images together, one of happiness, the other of anxiety, I'm in effect neutralizing the object of my fear.

Having stared your worst fears in the face and removed any bad feelings associated with them, you can now approach the job at hand in a completely relaxed, positive state of mind.

Try this method yourself. It really works for me, and it could help you too. We'll continue with more advanced quantum memory power techniques in the next chapter.

15

Your First Advanced Test

. . . .

Are you in the right frame of mind? We're going to have your first advanced test. I want you to prepare a journey of 30 stages. If you already have a route around your house, say of 10 stages, then just extend it further to 30. If it helps, write down the stages on a piece of paper so that you can get used to them and go through them a few times.

Make the stops interesting. Use a tree stump or a newspaper stand. Don't have too many stages that are all alike. If your journey takes you on a train, don't have more than 1 compartment. Make each stage unique. When you have all 30 stages, we'll begin the test.

Again, you can have someone read these directions to you, or record yourself and listen to the recording as you do this exercise.

I want you to get in the zone. You should be sitting upright, feet squarely on the ground, with a straight spine, head faced forward, hands on legs, and with a good, seated poise and a nice, straight back. You're feeling relaxed, and your breathing is smooth.

Close your eyes and picture yourself floating along your prepared journey. How should you see each stage? Try to take the same vantage point each time. Get a feel for each stage. It's not easy to explain the feelings you get from a room; it's a mixture of things. Associations from the past blend together to give you a unique feeling about a particular room. See if you can sense that.

Check your breathing. Make sure it's relaxed, but take in healthy breaths, in and out. Oxygen is vital for both your memory and your well-being. It promotes the growth of dendrites in the brain.

Progress along the journey, and feel your body relaxing all the time. Your mind shouldn't be racing. It should feel as if it's ticking over at a steady rate. It should be relaxed but focused.

If you noticed your eyelids are fluttering just slightly, that's a sign of the alpha wave. If you have that, you're in the perfect mode for concentrating, listening, and receiving information.

Once you think you know the route backwards and forwards, I'll start to give you the 30 objects in sequence. Here's what you should do: with your eyes closed, you should already be in position at the first stage. You're waiting for something to happen.

Again, use logic, but this time, also use slight exaggeration. You don't have to exaggerate the images too much, because they should already have become natural to you. Use color if you like. Make the picture instant—the first image that comes into your head, the first association. I'm not going to give you any help from now on. As you read each word or phrase, close your eyes and picture the object.

Here's the list:

Yellow balloon	Tape measure
Roses	Blue pen
Guitar	Briefcase
Teapot	Umbrella
Fluffy dog	Statue
Painting	Milk
Bus	Computer
Sandals	Wedding cake
Ice cream	Giraffe
Mirror	Pair of skis

Palm tree	Rope
Fishing rod	Golf bag
Hat	Sparkling dress
Hammer	Diary
Bag of diamonds	Fountain pen

Keep thinking all the time. Keep your eyes closed. Review the scenes. Return to the first stage, and work your way through. Keep calm; relax. Just let the images wash over you as they return. Don't force the memories. If you're not sure, just let it happen. If it doesn't come through, skip to the next stage.

SCORING YOURSELF

OK, do you have those images? Now write them down in order, and compare them to the list above. A score of 10 is excellent. If you can remember the first 7 in sequence, then you're in the top 1 percent of people with the best memories in the world.

If you've been practicing these techniques, then I'd expect a score of 10 to 20, which is excellent, particularly if they're in sequence. If you got a score of 20 to 25, then you are way above average. If you scored all 30, then you have me worried. Who are you? You could potentially be a major player in a national memory competition.

If for any reason you scored very badly, don't worry about it. Help is at hand. You just need to work on the visual side of your imagination a bit more.

People ask me, "How long does this information stay in your head?" Now you can be the judge. See how long that information stays in your head.

DEVELOPING YOUR POWERS OF VISUALIZATION

Here's an exercise to help you with your powers of visualization. Don't worry if you can't draw or if you're not very good at art.

Get hold of a vase of flowers or something similar. Get a piece of paper. Just study the vase of flowers for about 2 or 3 minutes, taking in as much detail as you can.

Then look away and just draw. Try to reproduce that vase of flowers in as much detail as you can. Spend a few minutes trying to do this. When you've run out of recollections, look at the vase of flowers again; this time you'll notice a bit more. You'll pick up maybe a shadow or the shape of the leaves.

Take in a bit more information. Study the vase of flowers again for another couple of minutes.

Then return to your drawing, and add those details in. Keep repeating this until you really run out of ideas. Try to remember as much detail as possible.

You should try this exercise on a regular basis. It really does help your observation as well as your powers of visualization.

16

Time Travel

. . . .

f you're frustrated by your inability to recall scenes from your childhood, this section is for you.

I suspect that we've all experienced that moment when happy memories of a previously forgotten part of our lives comes flooding back. It's an exciting feeling, but it can also be extremely frustrating. We can remember only bits of the past, little glimpses that rapidly fade into nothing.

I call this exercise "Time Travel," or "How to Remember Lost Chapters of Your Life." It's about returning to a particular time and location from your past and trying to recall everything in as much detail as you can.

Here's the technique: Start by mentally returning to a location that conjures up a number of varied, incidental recollections, like your old school or an old friend's house or a town you left long ago. Choose a specific starting point. It might be a flag-pole on the playground, a chapel pew, a tree hut, or a friend's kitchen.

Look around you. Think of the technique you used for remembering a picture. Throw yourself into the picture. Climb inside the frame. What little incidents do you remember? How old were you then? What friends did you have at the time? What were the typical noises? Traffic, trains, children playing?

Try to recall individual sounds, characteristics of particular objects, maybe the slam of a front door, a squeaky window, a creaky floorboard, or a water pipe that always shuddered. Perhaps you can recall the characteristic noises of places where you worked—a forklift, sliding doors, a photocopier, the now obsolete typewriter, or some sort of factory machinery.

Talking of factory machinery, I'm still haunted by the inimitable sounds of a heavy-duty shredding machine many years ago. For too long, my ears were subjected to the sound of splicing, ripping, and tearing as this monster relentlessly pulverized millions of square feet of photographic waste and negative film. All that noise for a few, small, silent bars of silver that were the end product. Even so, as I conjure up those unpleasant sounds from the past, I'm compensated by a flood of associated memories from that chapter of my life.

Happy associations are people, places, music, parties, and voices. See if you can recall voices, even their timbre. If you're using your old school or workplace as a location, try to remember catch phrases used by teachers and pupils or employers and workmates. Isolate particular events that took place. No matter how trivial they seem now, they obviously meant something to you then. As always, use all your senses.

Can you recall the smell of a damp, musty room or the aroma of your garden? What about the smooth feel of a polished walnut table or a rough texture of a brick wall—the one you used to run your hands along on the way to school?

You could slip an old record on a turntable to get yourself in the mood—maybe an old Beatles album or a Chopin classic. Music can act as a very powerful tool for remembering your past. It can propel you back to a distant time, with all the emotions, thoughts, and feelings that suddenly and uncannily return to you.

ASSOCIATION

Association is at the heart of time travel. One memory sparks off another, so after a while an overall picture begins to emerge, not just of the layout of a place, but also of your state of mind. Were you happy, optimistic, in love, depressed, or just naive?

The more deeply you reflect, the more memories will be triggered off. Experiences completely forgotten will come flooding back. Eventually, if you work hard at it, you'll have the same problem as I have. I never run out of memories.

Try to make this a daily routine. Spend a little time every day reflecting on the same area of your past until you feel you've exhausted every avenue of retrieval. It's possible you never will. Every time you return to the scene, you'll be starting with a clearer, more comprehensive picture. It's a bit like assembling a jigsaw puzzle: each detail adds something to the overall picture.

Here are some other benefits. Time travel borders on self-hypnosis, but it comes with no health warnings, and you won't need the click of someone's fingers to wake you. When I relax in my sauna of early childhood memories, I adopt the same frame of mind I had all those years ago: carefree, innocent, untroubled. Only then do I realize how much my expectations and opinions have changed.

Time travel has many other benefits. One common symptom of people who don't know how to use their memories is a failure to recall dreams.

It's nonsense to say that we don't dream. We all dream every night. It's the brain's way of filing the thoughts it had during the day. By exercising your memory regularly, you'll begin to recall more and more dreams. You might even have more wild and untamed dreams.

Finally, you may wish to use the findings of your archeological dig for the journey method. When I memorized 40 decks of cards, I needed 40 separate journeys. Many of them were taken from my childhood.

Just as athletes train to get into the zone, so you should try to be aware of setting your brain to the desired frequencies for learning and memory. Practice relaxation, and imagine slowing down your brain waves. High-frequency brain waves are reserved for excitement and the fun fair.

If you want to be an Einstein, then slow down just a little. If you're feeling stressed and the pressure is on, then practice the relaxation exercises I've given above. You'll find it easier to create images and recall old memories. Have fun traveling back in time. Your memories are important. They define you. Isn't it worth revisiting the best parts of your life?

17

Card Memorization

At this point we're going to turn up the degree of difficulty. If you're getting on well with this book and finding the tests and exercises easy, then watch out. The final tests in these sessions are as tough as they get.

If you've been successful in memorizing 10 objects in sequence, then there's nothing to stop you from memorizing 50 or more objects. It's just that the speed needs to catch up a little bit. That will follow when you practice.

If you're able to memorize 50 objects in sequence, then a 100-digit number should be no problem to you because you have a newly trained memory. All it takes is confidence, organization, the will, and the desire to succeed, and of course, a bit of imagination.

What I'm trying to get at is you're probably already a memory champion. Perhaps you're
a potential World Memory Champion. If you are,
you're going to have to learn how to memorize a
deck of cards.

Perhaps you like to play card games like bridge,
whist, poker, or blackjack. Maybe you'd like to
memorize a pack of cards, or you're just curious to
know how it's done. Whatever you may think, card
memorizing is, I believe, once of the most elegant
exercises for fine-tuning your memory.

A few years ago at the World Memory Championships, I won the event for memorizing the most
decks of cards in 1 hour, and that was 18½ decks,
or 962 playing cards. The strange thing is that
in 1987, I couldn't string more than about 5 or 6
playing cards together.

The technique I use is being implemented by
most of my major competitors. I don't know any
major rival that doesn't use some form of journey
method to memorize playing cards. Certainly all of
them translate the cards into symbolic images. As
far as I know, none of the top memorizers memorize by brute force memory. It just doesn't happen.
They have to use some sort of strategy. I think the
most efficient way to memorize a deck of cards is
as follows.

I have a deck right here. I'll give them a quick shuffle. Now I'm just going to file through the deck here. As I thumb through the cards, they jump out at me. I have the jack of hearts here. That's my Uncle Jim. The ace of diamonds, that's John Cleese from Monty Python. The 9 of clubs: golfer Nick Faldo. The 7 of spades is a friend of mine called Terry, and the 6 of spades is my girlfriend. It goes on and on like that.

It's become automatic for me. I really don't have to work at it anymore, but I did originally. How did I arrive at these characters? I started off by looking at the court cards. I picked out the jacks, kings, queens, and I started looking at their faces. I thought, "Well, the king reminds me of a friend of mine. He's a bit rotund." Then I saw vague resemblances to old girlfriends, uncles, friends, and famous people.

I suggest you get out a deck of cards and do the same thing. Just work on the court cards to begin with: the kings, the jacks, the queens, all 12 of them, and see whom they remind you of. I tend to stick to the same pack of cards, just as a golfer sticks to his favorite putter or a tennis player likes to play with a certain weighted racket.

Keep going through the deck until you recognize the cards as people. Once you've done that, start to look at other cards. Do any of those cards trigger a particular person? For me, the 7 of hearts is James Bond, 007 heartthrob. How about the 10 of spades? Again, that's Dudley Moore, because he was in the film *10*. How about 6? It's sort of a sexy sounding card. Who is your 6 of hearts?

Let your creative mind supply you with associations. If you really can't find a link between the card and a familiar face, then help is at hand. You can always resort to the Dominic system. I've enabled you to translate the suits into letters in the following way.

For clubs, take the first letter, C. Clubs is C, diamonds is D, hearts is H, and spades is S. Fairly straightforward. Now you can get initials of famous people or friends. Remember the code for the Dominic system? 1 is A, 2 is B, 3 is C, and so on. So what would the 2 of clubs translate to? Think about it. BC: Bing Crosby. How about the 2 of hearts? That could give you BH: Benny Hill or Bob Hope.

What about the 4 of clubs? That gives you DC, David Copperfield, the magician. How about the 3 of spades? CS, Claudia Schiffer. That could be an interesting combination, the 4 of clubs and the 3 of spades.

For the 9 of diamonds, here's a good one: ND, Neil Diamond. The 3 of hearts, CH, actor Charlton

Heston. Before you even attempt to memorize a deck of cards, you have to learn the language first. When you deal a card, you should see a person, to the point where it becomes automatic.

Think about typists. Does a professional typist have to look down at the keyboard? No. His or her fingers know exactly where to go, just like those of a pianist. It's the same thing with cards. When you see a 3 of spades, you see Claudia Schiffer; 9 of diamonds, Neil Diamond; 2 of hearts, Benny Hill.

To reinforce the image, give that person a prop and an action. Jim, my uncle, the jack of hearts, is always reading *The Times* newspaper. The 9 of clubs is Nick Faldo, who's always swinging his golf club. Any chance he gets, he'll practice his swing, being the perfectionist he is.

This is very useful because you want your characters and actions to be versatile. You want them to fit in in any situation, any location. Faldo, the 9 of clubs, must be allowed to swing his club anywhere he likes, just as Jim must read his paper wherever he wants.

Take the example of the ace of diamonds, which for me is always John Cleese. I'm not exactly sure how I arrived at this. It may be because the ace looks tall. Anyway, I have the image of John Cleese sitting behind a news desk.

If you've ever watched the old Monty Python sketches, occasionally Cleese would be behind his desk in all sorts of different locations. His favorite catch line was, "And now for something completely different." He could be on the top or even the side of a cliff, but I think my favorite one was when they put the desk in the sea. It was floating in the sea, and he was dressed up to the nines as a typical newscaster with a tie on, saying, "And now for something completely different."

You can see how useful these persons and their actions and props can be, because you can put them absolutely anywhere. The 3 of spades is Claudia Schiffer. She's always striding a catwalk, with her hands on her hips. The 4 of clubs, David Copperfield, is always pulling a rabbit out of a hat or flying. What about the 2 of clubs, Bing Crosby? He's always decorating a Christmas tree and singing "White Christmas."

Do you see what's happening here? The characters are becoming animated. You've breathed life into the cards, and now you have something you can work with.

A JOURNEY OF 52 STAGES

You know what's coming up. You're going to form a journey of 52 stages. Once you see a person every time a card comes up, and you have your journey of 52 stages sorted out, all you have to do is put the two together.

Don't run before you can walk. Start with half a deck or even with 10 playing cards. Use a journey of 10 stages, and imagine bumping into 10 famous royal, political people, whatever it is, doing what they do best.

For example, here's a typical short journey for you. The first stage of the journey is the front gate of my old school. I'm there standing at the front gate, and now I deal the first card. It's the 2 of clubs, Bing Crosby. He's decorating a Christmas tree. Got that?

Now I go to the second stage of my journey, and I'm looking at playing fields on my right, because something is going to happen there. I deal the next card. It's the 9 of clubs. Immediately I think of Nick Faldo practicing his golf swing.

Now I go to the third stage of my journey, and I'm in a corridor in my school. Next card: 3 of spades. That's Claudia Schiffer. She's striding up and down the corridor, giving the schoolboys a treat.

Next one, fourth stage, I'm in the chemistry lab. What do I see now? The 4 of clubs. That's David Copperfield. He's flying around the lab.

Go to the fifth stage. I'm in the library. Deal the fifth card, and it's the 9 of diamonds. Who's that?

It's Neil Diamond. He's sitting on a rock, singing, "Love on the Rocks." Nobody in the library can concentrate or study. He's about to be thrown out.

You see what's happening. You just go on and on, attaching cards as people to the various locations along your journey.

A quick recap. Go back to the first stage, outside the gate. Who's there decorating a tree? Bing Crosby: 2 of clubs. Second stage, to my right I see Nick Faldo: 9 of clubs.

Go into the corridor. Who's that? Claudia Schiffer. It has to be the 3 of spades. Go to the fourth stage, into the chemistry lab: 4 of clubs. It has to be David Copperfield. Fifth stage: Neil Diamond.

Notice that I'm not making a story. I'm merely connecting each character to a stage along a journey, so I don't have to connect Bing Crosby to Nick Faldo. They're not even within earshot. They're just connected to the background. I'm not making a story, but I am making a logical connection; I'm using reason. It may be bizarre to have Neil Diamond singing in the library, but it's possible. What are the consequences? What are the chances of Claudia Schiffer striding up and down the corridor of my old school? Highly unlikely, but what if? What are the consequences?

You're probably thinking, "Yes, but I could never get down to 30 seconds. There's so much to do." Yet my very first deck took me 26 minutes, and I made about 25 errors, and that's after I had associations for all the cards. You could easily get down to 5 minutes or lower. If you can, you're probably about one in a million.

To recap: learn the language. To begin with, pull out the court cards. Whom do the illustrations remind you of? Do any of the cards, like the 7 of hearts, prompt or trigger a person? Use the Dominic system to translate cards into initials of famous people or family or a friend. Give each character an associated prop, an action. Nick Faldo has golf clubs. David Copperfield is always performing magic.

Before you attempt to memorize a deck, deal through it until you can recognize each card as a person performing their unique action.

To memorize a deck of 52 cards, you need a mental journey of 52 stages or stops. Get to know the journey inside out. Remember, the journey preserves the order of the information you're about to absorb. Put it all together. Shuffle the deck, and slowly deal out each card as you post them to stages that follow the sequence of your journey.

Animate the scenes. Use color, logic, exaggeration, humor, sex. Use all your senses. Use all your cortical skills. Remember the ideal conditions. Relax, slow down your brain waves. The mere act of mentally seeing these imagined scenes will encourage brain wave control and balance.

Make sure you time your very first deck. It's a great feeling to have mastered your first deck. It doesn't matter if it takes you an hour. You can rest assured that the next time you'll dramatically cut down that time. In the space of 3 months, I went from 26 minutes and 25 errors to 70 seconds with no errors.

USEFUL TIPS

Here are some useful tips. Make sure the journey is solid. Always get yourself in position before you deal a card. You're already in the bedroom in the first stage, ready for the first card. If you find it difficult to imagine at the outset, try closing your eyes as soon as each card is dealt. Remember, with your eyes shut, you promote alpha and theta waves and you're blocking out distractions. It's easier to concentrate and visualize.

Another tip: imagine that the area is quiet initially. If you're in a town, float through it, and imagine it's a ghost town. All the inhabitants have disappeared. The ghost town is about to be brought to life by the characters who are about to materialize through your imagination. A Roman author writing 2,000 years ago had exactly the same advice: "It is better to form one's memory loci in a deserted and solitary place, for crowds of passing people tend to weaken the impressions."

Although you might think you simply don't know enough locations to store all the information you need, your imagination will ensure that you never run out, because as the ancient author says, "Even a person who thinks that he does not possess enough sufficiently good loci can remedy this, for thought can embrace any region whatsoever, and in it and at will, construct the setting of some place."

This author was saying that you can use imaginary settings. You could create an infinite number of imaginary places in your mind to house your mnemonic images. The Greeks employed a healthy mixture of fictitious places as well as real ones, and they often combined the two. For example, if there aren't enough rooms in your house to make a route that's long enough, you could always create an extra floor or dig out a basement. Anything is possible, and of course you don't need to apply for a permit.

A word on visualization: Believe it or not, I don't see an image in immaculate detail. I cannot reproduce perfect internal images. I suspect I do when I'm dreaming, but not when I'm memorizing. Anyway, I don't need that much detail for the image to stick in my mind.

Think about this. If I said to you now, "Don't look around, but Nelson Mandela is standing behind you," you have enough of an internal image to picture him. You don't need a faithfully reproduced image; you know he's standing there. Just a few reminders: that characteristic voice, that pleasant face, a flash of gray hair here and there. That's all you need to know that Nelson Mandela is standing there behind you. Of course, that's where logic kicks in. What the hell is he doing there anyway?

So please don't feel that visualization is the be-all and end-all to imagination. Use whatever works: sound, taste, touch, movement, exaggeration, and so on. Imagination is a combination of all these things.

INCREASING YOUR STORAGE CAPACITY

At this point you may think it's feasible to memorize a deck of cards, even in 5 minutes, but how do you memorize 40 decks in one go?

When I initially practiced with cards a number of years ago, I found that the journey method was so powerful that if I used the same journey a second time, I got a sort of double image. If I tried to memorize another deck of cards, I still had the first series of cards in my head. So I thought, "I'm going to have to invent a second journey here," because it was taking about 24 hours for some of these images to dissolve. Then I found that I needed a third route, and then a fourth, fifth, and sixth. What happened was when I got up to 6 decks, my storage capacity went from 52 to 312 stages. That meant I could memorize 312 shopping items, a list of 312 names, 312 pairs of numbers, and so on—312 of anything. It was a bit like disk space on a computer. To memorize 40 decks of cards, I had to prepare 40 separate journeys, each consisting of 52 stages. That's when I got real storage space: it went up to 2,080 stages.

With this amount of storage capacity, I can do a lot of the World Memory Championships, and I need this capacity, because these are some of the events: You have 2,000 digits to memorize in an hour. You have multiple decks of cards to memorize in an hour. You have names and faces, abstract images, and 300 random words. It goes on and on.

Probably the most difficult one—and this is where you have to control your stress—is the spoken number test. You're listening to a recording, and you hear a voice call out 400 digits at the rate of 1 digit every 2 seconds: 6, 8, 3, and so on.

Even if you're successful in memorizing 400 digits, if you get the second digit wrong, your score is 1. It's sudden death.

A NUMBERS TEST

I'm not going to give you a 400-digit number, but I'm going to give you a 30-digit number to memorize, and it's going to be at the rate of 1 digit every 2 seconds. The average recall for this test is about 7 or 8 digits, which indicates an average IQ. If you can go to more than 9 or 10, that indicates a high IQ. If you're anywhere near 30, then your IQ is through the roof. So here's an instant IQ raiser for you.

The first step is preparing yourself. Before you start, get organized. How are you going to attempt this task? Are you going to look at doing 2 digits at a time, or are you going to use number shapes, or number rhymes to do 1 digit at a time? So you're either going to have to have a 15-stage journey or a 30-stage journey.

Again, you can either have someone else read out this number list, or you can record yourself saying them, at a rate of 1 for every 2 seconds, and play them back. Here they are: 7, 9, 2, 2, 6, 4, 0, 1, 7, 8, 4, 0, 0, 3, 5, 3, 9, 6, 0, 9, 1, 5, 4, 0, 3, 2, 6, 6, 6, 3.

Keep thinking all the time. Write your answers down on a piece of paper, as we do at the World Memory Championships. When you're finished, look at the numbers as printed above, and make a note of your score.

How did you fare? What was your score? If you got 7 right, then that indicates an average IQ. If you got 10 to 15, that shows a high IQ; 16 to 25 right, then we're talking genius level. If you got 26 to 30, you're one in a million, and you should think about competing.

Now comes the postmortem. If you made a mistake, why? After a while, you may notice that certain numbers or playing cards or even objects always seem to trip you up. You may also find that one or two stages of a journey somehow don't seem to work either. This is where analyzing the result is so beneficial. Which symbols are causing you trouble? Maybe they're not strong enough for you. Then replace them. Perhaps a feature of the journey is so uninteresting that it's no wonder the images don't stick to it; in which case, just rearrange the journey. Reroute it. It's a type of delayed biofeedback.

Another pointer: if you slow down on your progress, then you should try and get faster. You should try and make mistakes. I can remember one of the English competitors gave me a call once. She said, "I can never seem to get below 4 minutes for a deck of cards."

"How many mistakes are you making on 4 minutes?" I asked.

"I never make a mistake."

"That's your problem. You have to start making mistakes. You have to push it."

Every time I practice, I usually try to get down to about 30 seconds or below. I make sure I always make about 4 or 5 errors. Otherwise, if I'm having perfect recall every time, I'm not really pushing myself; I don't know where my limits are.

18

Becoming a Mentathlete

. . . .

Competitors who take part in mind sports, whether it's chess, memory, bridge, speed reading, and so on are now being referred to as *mentathletes*. With prize money and world titles at stake, these mentathletes are beginning to train, just like any other top athletes, from tennis, swimming, skiing to motor racing or football.

Athletes of all kinds are increasingly turning their attention toward their brains. Top golfers now employ therapists, mentors, and mind gurus. My guru is the brain wave machine. Balance is the name of the game, and this latest technology helps you to achieve it. It involves wearing a pair of glasses with LEDs or light-emitting diodes, which pulsate at varying speeds.

At the same time, you wear a set of headphones, which produce a beat in time with the lights, so the effect of this combination of light and sound trains the brain to tune in to the optimum frequencies for learning, concentration, memory, and relaxation whilst at the same time balancing the brain waves of both hemispheres.

I believe that in the future not only will we see sportsmen and women utilizing this technology, but it will become a requirement in industry and education that's available for everyone. Of course, you can help to balance your own brain anytime you want just by memorizing a shopping list.

A DAY IN THE LIFE

Now you know pretty much all there is to know about the strategies that we professional memory men and women employ to win competitions. Maybe you're thinking that you should enter yourself, but these days the sport of memory is growing into a serious business. The winners of the national championships are guaranteed exposure on television and on magazines in their own countries, and they do radio interviews as well. Some of them even have agents.

Such is the competition these days that I now have to prepare and train harder, not because my memory isn't working so well, but because the competition is getting stronger. More countries are starting their own championships, so the best are sent to England to compete for the world title (which, I hasten to add, I intend to hang on to for quite some time).

As part of my training, I also look to my body, usually a couple of months before. Here's an idea of the training that I have to do. In 1991, all I had to do was take a week's vacation to practice for the World Memory Championships, which I won. However, in 2000, I had to devote the preceding two months solely to training in order to give myself a chance of winning the title again.

Such is the competition these days that I'm having to train for longer and harder. During that tough period of memory training, this is a typical day's schedule.

I wake up at 8:00, and the first thing I do is try and recall the previous night's dreams. I do this just to get my visualization going. At 9:00, I do five minutes' physical warm-up exercises. At five minutes past 9:00, I'll go for a 4-mile cross-country run. Then, at 10:00, I'll spend 10 minutes on a brain wave balancing machine. This is sophisticated optical and acoustical equipment, which helps to balance my brain.

Half past 10:00, I'll have a light breakfast, but I'll also take a tablet of gingko biloba, which helps to improve the circulation. At 11:00, typically I'll memorize a 1,000-digit number. At half past 11:00, I connect my brain up to an EEG at this time, and I perform about a one-hour biofeedback session.

Half past 12:00, I'll do another half-hour EEG testing, and at the same time, I practice visualization techniques and meditation as well. At 1:00, I'll have a bit of lunch and relaxation. At 2:00, I might go out and play a bit of golf, either a full round or just a quick half round game.

At 6:00, I'll have a glass of fresh orange juice. No alcohol throughout the 2 months of training. At 7:00, a fast sprint of playing card memorization. In other words, I'll go through a deck of cards as fast as I can. Half past 7:00, dinner; at 8:00, I'll have about an hour's brain training with a virtual reality computer game.

At 9:00, I work with a specially designed computer program which knocks out random decimals, random words, binary digits, and many more things. At 10:00, I'll relax, maybe watch a film, and then, around 1:00 in the morning, sweet dreams.

A FINAL TEST

Time for another test. This time I'm going to give you a list of 30 names. It's not sudden death; I just want you to try to memorize as many as you can in sequence. Use all the mental tools available to you. Prepare another journey, or use one from an earlier session. You've probably developed two or three journeys by now. Remember, the more journeys you have, the more storage space you'll develop.

Again, you can either have someone read this list aloud to you, or you can record yourself reading it and play it back.

Listen to each name, and let that name trigger somebody you know or somebody famous, and associate that person with the background of the journey that you have. Of course, you'll need a journey with 30 stages.

Here come those 30 names: Robert, Lucy, Caroline, Edward, Monica, Pamela, Jim, Sally, Rupert, Sam, Rosy, Judd, Sharon, Elvis, David, Madonna, Mike, Dominic, Rebecca, Allen, Jessie, Max, Sarah, Henry, Claudia, Peter, Jenny, Mary, Charles, Elizabeth.

Keep thinking all the time. Let the images wash over you.

I did warn you these tests were going to be tough. I want you to make sure you have those names along your journey, so play through them again quickly, or have your friend read them to you. When you've finished, write down the names in order, and make a note of your score.

I'm going to give you a list of 30 objects now, and I want you to connect those names to their corresponding objects.

So, for example, when you go back to the first stage, you'll be seeing Robert in your mind's eye. I'm gong to feed you with *blue socks*. You have to imagine Robert putting on blue socks or doing something with the blue socks. Every time you hear a description, you have to connect that person with the object. Got the idea?

Here goes: blue socks, magazine, microphone, hand grenade, cigar, tennis racket, snoring, fishing rod, hammer, basketball, telescope, dance, naked, hair dryer, hamburger, kissing, boxing gloves, piano, painting, hysterical, flying, drunk, lipstick, rude noise, card game, guitar, fur coat, anesthetic, golf club, and barbecue.

Now here is the list of the person and the corresponding object, so you can determine your score.

Robert, blue socks	Rupert, hammer
Lucy, magazine	Sam, basketball
Caroline, microphone	Rosy, telescope
Edward, hand grenade	Judd, dance
Monica, cigar	Sharon, naked
Pamela, tennis racket	Elvis, hair dryer
Jim, snoring	David, hamburger
Sally, fishing rod	Madonna, kissing

Mike, boxing gloves

Dominic, piano

Rebecca, painting

Allen, hysterical

Jessie, flying

Max, drunk

Sarah, lipstick

Henry, rude noise

Claudia, card game

Peter, guitar

Jenny, fur coat

Mary, anesthetic

Charles, golf club

Elizabeth, barbecue

I'll bet you had a lot of fun with that list.

Calculate your score. If you got 5 to 10, that's about average for this test. If you got 11 to 20, you're way above average; 21 to 30, then you're talking genius level. You have a vibrant imagination. If you scored really badly, don't worry. Just keep practicing. You'll get there.

19

Final Thoughts

. . . .

Congratulations on completing *Quantum Memory Power*! If just one aspect of your memory has been improved, whether it's absorbing names or telephone numbers more easily or the ability to remember a simple shopping list, then studying this course has been more than worthwhile. Kick-starting your memory in one area will create a chain reaction of organized thought, with all the benefits that go with it.

The path to developing quantum memory power lies before you. It's not an exclusive path, with access granted only to those with a special gift for learning. It is, instead, available to anyone and everyone who has a brain, and that means you.

You are well equipped with an incredible potential for absorbing knowledge. Let your imagination—the key to learning and memory—unleash that brain power and propel you along at ever-increasing speeds. Practice your newfound skills using those three inseparable tools: association, location, and imagination. Use number shapes, and in particular the Dominic system, to help you digest and demystify awkward items that you need to know: PIN numbers, telephone numbers, dates, statistics, foreign words, playing cards, names, and faces. They can all be processed swiftly and filed away neatly once you know how to convert them easily into colorful, meaningful, and memorable images.

Of course, the more you practice, the sooner these skills will become second nature to you. The techniques, systems, and methods I've given you in this book have been developed from experience. They have served me very well, and I for one would be lost without them. They're the result of a process of selection that has taken over 30 years of research to develop. They are yours now to take full advantage of. Apply them, and you will reap more than just the benefits of owning a reliable and efficient memory. You will require an insatiable appetite for learning. Maybe one of these days you'll be challenging me for the title of World Memory Champion. Good luck!

www.ingramcontent.com/pod-product-compliance
Lightning Source LLC
Jackson TN
JSHW011934131224
75386JS00041B/1375

* 9 7 8 1 7 2 2 5 0 3 2 4 6 *